POETRY FOR UKRAINE

Poetry in support of Ukraine,
from poets around the world.

Compiled by Robin Barratt

Published by THE POET

Poetry For Ukraine

ISBN:9798447088378

© THE POET, April 2022, and all the authors herein

All rights reserved. No part of this publication may be reproduced,
distributed, or transmitted in any form or by any means,
including photocopying, recording, or other electronic or mechanical methods,
without the prior written permission of the publisher,
except in the case of brief quotations embodied in critical reviews and
certain other non-commercial uses permitted by copyright law.
For permission requests, email the publisher at the address below.

E: Robin@ThePoetMagazine.org

Cover image and design: Canva
www.Canva.com

Compiled and published for THE POET by:
Robin Barratt Publishing
Affordable Publishing Services

www.RobinBarratt.co.uk

THANK YOU!

To compile and publish an anthology with so many contributors, so quickly, was a mammoth task, and without the support of our sponsors and donations, we could never have got **POETRY FOR UKRAINE** off the ground, compiled and published so quickly. So a **VERY BIG THANK YOU** to everyone below ...

Sponsors:

John Johnson (VIRGINIA, USA)
Poems Over Coffee - www.PoemsOverCoffee.com

Mary Keating Esq, LLC (CONNECTICUT, USA)
www.MKeatinglaw.com

Dr Sarah & David Clarke - LONDON, ENGLAND.

Donations:

Kelly Madden (CANADA), **Jeffrey Marshall** (USA), **James Coburn** (USA), **Margaret Duda** (USA), **Rhonda Parsons** (USA), **Suzan Denis** (CANADA), **Roy Adams** (CANADA), **Stephen Poole** (ENGLAND), **Sara Sarna** (USA), **Mark Fleisher** (USA), **Carol Tahir** (USA), **Jocelyn Boor** (USA), **Denise Steele** (USA), **Judith Brickner** (USA), **Gordon Simmonds** (REPUBLIC OF IRELAND), **Adrienne Stevenson** (USA), **Tamam Kahn** (USA), **Sally Zakariya** (USA), **Anna Marie Dunlap** (USA), **Carol Seitchik** (USA), **Eric Forsbergh** (USA), **Louis Faber** (USA), **Matteo Marangoni** (ITALY), **Marilyn Peretti** (USA), **Larry Jaffe** (USA), **Akua Lezli Hope** (USA), and the **Migrant Workers of Hong Kong**. And also, thank you to **Bronwyn Vanzino** (AUSTRALIA) for your continued support for **THE POET**.

If you would like to sponsor the **POETRY FOR UKRAINE** website, or donate, please go to the website below and click on **SUPPORT US**

www.PoetryForUkraine.org

FB: @PoetryForUkraine
Instagram: @PoetryForUkraine

We have had submissions to *POETRY FOR UKRAINE* from around the world, and for a number of poets contributing to this collection, English is not their first language. Unlike other poetry platforms and publications, we do not heavily edit a poet's own work (*if we did, it would then not be their own work!*), so please focus on a poet's message and heartfelt support for Ukraine, and the meaning of their poetry, and not necessarily on any grammatical mistakes or translated imperfections.

CONTENTS

Abdumominov Abdulloh (UZBEKISTAN) ... page 143
Abigail George (SOUTH AFRICA) ... page 234
Adrienne Stevenson (CANADA) ... page 69
Agnieszka Filipek (REPUBLIC OF IRELAND / POLAND) ... page 236
Agnieszka Wiktorowska-Chmielewska (POLAND) ... page 237
Akua Lezli Hope (USA) ... page 274
Alex Chornyj (CANADA) ... page 169
Alex Hand (AUSTRALIA) ... page 44
Alfredo Quarto (USA) ... page 56
Dr. Alicia Minjarez Ramirez (MEXICO) ... page 167
Alicja Maria Kuberska (POLAND) ... page 96
Amelia Fielden (AUSTRALIA) ... page 30
Amit Parmessur (MAURITIUS) ... page 238
Amrita Valan (INDIA) ... page 239
Anamika Nandy (INDIA) ... page 197
Andrea Carter Brown (USA) ... page 173
Ann Privateer (USA) ... page 62
Anna Dunlap (USA) ... page 241
Anne Maureen Medrano Esperidion (HONG KONG) ... page 67
Anne Mitchell (USA) ... page 68
Annie Wright (SCOTLAND) ... page 55
Arbër Selmani (KOSOVO) ... page 60
Ayesha Khurram (PAKISTAN) ... page 99
Barry Pittard (AUSTRALIA) ... page 101
Beata B. Agustin (PHILIPPINES) ... page 100
Beckham Lim (SINGAPORE) ... page 26
Beverly M. Collins (USA) ... page 118
Bhuwan Thapaliya (NEPAL) ... page 78
Bill Cushing (USA) ... page 242
Binod Dawadi (NEPAL) ... page 126
Bobby Z (USA) ... page 121
Bozena Helena Mazur-Nowak (ENGLAND / POLAND) ... page 86
Brajesh Singh (INDIA) ... page 83
Brian Wake (ENGLAND) ... page 247
Bruce W. Niedt (USA) ... page 84
Bryan Franco (USA) ... page 245
Carol Moeke (ENGLAND) ... page 39
Carol Parris Krauss (USA) ... page 28
Carol Seitchik (USA) ... page 141
Carol Tahir (USA) ... page 248
Carole Stone (USA) ... page 54
Caroline Johnson (USA) ... page 31
Cathy Cade (ENGLAND) ... page 22
Cathy Hailey (USA) ... page 228

Chad Norman (CANADA) ... page 91
Charo Gabay Sidon (SINGAPORE/ PHILIPPINES) ... page 105
Chester Civelli (SWITZERLAND) ... page 88
Christine Aurelio (HONG KONG / PHILIPPINES) ... page 145
Christopher Bogart (USA) ... page 97
Chrys Salt MBE (ENGLAND / SCOTLAND) ... page 49
Chua Rui Heng (SINGAPORE) ... page 249
Colette Tennant (USA) ... page 151
Cordelia M. Hanemann (USA) ... page 180
Craven L. Sutton, Jr. (USA) ... page 38
Cynthia Atkin (USA) ... page 124
Daniel de Culla (SPAIN) ... page 71
David Dephy (USA / GEORGIA) ... page 19
David Sparenberg (USA) ... page 47
David Webb (ENGLAND) ... page 13
Debi Schmitz Noriega (USA) ... page 282
Deborah Hefferon (USA) ... page 102
Denise Steele (SCOTLAND) ... page 181
DeWitt Clinton (USA) ... page 182
Djehane Hassouna (USA) ... page 157
Don Beukes (SOUTH AFRICA / ENGLAND) ... page 250
Donna Zephrine (USA) ... page 251
Ed Ruzicka (USA) ... page 131
Eduard Schmidt-Zorner (REPUBLIC OF IRELAND) ... page 29
Eithne Cullen (ENGLAND / REPUBLIC OF IRELAND) ... page 117
Eleni Vasiliou-Asteroskoni (GERMANY / GREECE) ... page 58
Eliza Segiet (POLAND) ... page 36
Elizabeth Harmatys Park (USA) ... page 285
Elizabeth Sophia Strauss (USA) ... page 165
Elsie Isayas Calumpiano (SINGAPORE / PHILIPPINES) ... page 176
Eric Forsbergh (USA) ... page 41
Eric Lawson (USA) ... page 74
Ermira Mitre Kokomani (USA / ALBANIA) ... page 174
Estelle Phillips (ENGLAND) ... page 106
Ewith Bahar (INDONESIA) ... page 252
Fahredin Shehu (KOSOVO) ... page 73
Finola Scott (SCOTLAND) ... page 148
Fiona Owen (WALES) ... page 155
Francisc Edmund Balogh (ROMANIA) ... page 119
Fred Johnston (REPUBLIC OF IRELAND) ... page 70
Gary Beck (USA) ... page 178
Gary Shulman, MS. Ed (USA) ... page 77
Geoff Ward (REPUBLIC OF IRELAND / ENGLAND) ... page 139
Geoffrey Heptonstall (ENGLAND) ... page 21
George O. Ndukwu (NIGERIA) ... page 253
Germain Droogenbroodt (SPAIN / BELGIUM) ... page 166

Gloria Sofia (NETHERLANDS / CAPE VERDE) ... page 108
Gordon J Simmonds (ENGLAND) ... page 85
Hein Min Tun (MYANMAR) ... page 177
Hema Savithri (INDIA) ... page 254
Hillol Ray (USA) ... page 114
Hussein Habasch (KURDISTAN) ... page 20
Igor Pop Trajkov (NORTH MACEDONIA) ... page 132
Irma Kurti (ITALY / ALBANIA) ... page 113
Ivana Radojičić (SERBIA) ... page 128
Jack Henry (USA) ... page 24
Jake Cosmos Aller (SOUTH KOREA / USA) ... page 159
James A. Carter (USA) ... page 66
James Aitchison (AUSTRALIA) ... page 23
James Coburn (USA) ... page 16
Janelyn Dupingay Vergara (SINGAPORE / PHILIPPINES) ... page 33
Jasna Šamić (FRANCE / BOSNIA & HERZEGOVINA) ... page 25
Jason Kirk Bartley (USA) ... page 80
Javisth Bhugobaun (MAURITIUS) ... page 90
Jeffrey Marshall (USA) ... page 255
Joan McNerney (USA) ... page 59
Jocelyn Boor (USA) ... page 53
John Davis (USA) ... page 122
John Notley (THAILAND / ENGLAND) ... page 150
John Tunaley (ENGLAND) ... page 179
Jonathan Ukah (ENGLAND / NIGERIA) ... page 45
Joralyn Fallera Mounsel (SINGAPORE / PHILIPPINES) ... page 183
Jose Manoj Mathews T (INDIA) ... page 127
Joseph A. Farina (CANADA) ... page 32
Judy Jones Brickner (USA) ... page 64
Julia Paulette Hollenbery (ENGLAND) ... page 283
Jyotirmaya Thakur (ENGLAND / INDIA) ... page 135
Kakoli Ghosh (INDIA) ... page 256
Karen Douglass (USA) ... page 95
Karyn J. Powers (USA) ... page 257
Kate Young (ENGLAND) ... page 184
Kathrine Yets (USA) ... page 186
Kathy Sherban (CANADA) ... page 258
Kavita Ezekiel Mendonca (CANADA / INDIA) ... page 63
Keith Burton (USA) ... page 260
Keith Jepson (ENGLAND) ... page 187
Kelly Madden (CANADA) ... page 52
Kerfe Roig (USA) ... page 209
Kirsty Niven (SCOTLAND) ... page 15
Krishna Kumar Srinivasan (INDIA) ... page 81
Larry Jaffe (USA) ... page 14
Laura Felleman (USA) ... page 189

Lauren Mosher (USA) ... page 259
Lily Swarn (INDIA) ... page 109
Linda M. Crate (USA) ... page 191
Lorraine Sicelo Mangena (ZIMBABWE) ... page 190
Louis Faber (USA) ... page 149
Low Kian Seh (SINGAPORE) ... page 120
Lucinda Trew (USA) ... page 193
Lynette G. Esposito (USA) ... page 261
Lynn White (WALES) ... page 46
Dr. Lynne Sedgmore CBE (ENGLAND) ... page 35
Ma Jolie Fille (SINGAPORE / INDONESIA) ... page 262
Manju Kanchuli Tiwari (NEPAL) ... page 281
Mantas Stočkus (MALTA / LITHUANIA) ... page 134
Mantz Yorke (ENGLAND) ... page 192
Margaret Duda (USA) ... page 171
Margarita Vanyova Dimitrova (BULGARIA) ... page 185
Maria Editha Garma-Respicio (HONG KONG / PHILIPPINES) ... page 125
Maria Nemy Lou Rocio (HONG KONG / PHILIPPINES) ... page 271
Marianne Peel (USA) ... page 194
Marie C. Lecrivain (USA) ... page 196
Marilyn Peretti (USA) ... page 288
Marjorie Gowdy (USA) ... page 198
Mark Andrew Heathcote (ENGLAND) ... page 199
Mark Fleisher (USA) ... page 206
Mark Saba (USA) ... page 201
Martha Fox (USA) ... page 204
Martin Milmo (ENGLAND) ... page 202
Martyn Hesford (ENGLAND) ... page 50
Mary Ellen Fean (REPUBLIC OF IRELAND) ... page 208
Mary Keating (USA) ... page 264
Masudul Hoq (BANGLADESH) ... page 265
Matteo Marangoni (ITALY) ... page 266
Meenakshi Palaniappan (SINGAPORE) ... page 267
Melissa Miles (NEW ZEALAND) ... page 269
Meri Utkovska (REPUBLIC OF NORTH MACEDONIA) ... page 270
Michael Rollins (ENGLAND) ... page 286
Michael Claxton (JAPAN) ... page 87
Michael H. Brownstein (USA) ... page 278
Michelle Morris (ENGLAND) ... page 276
Moinak Dutta (INDIA) ... page 279
Monsif Beroual (MOROCCO) ... page 290
Moushumi Bhattacharjee (INDIA) ... page 289
Naida Mujkić (BOSNIA AND HERZEGOVINA) ... page 291
Nancy Byrne Iannucci (USA) ... page 153
Nandita De (INDIA) ... page 292
Naseha Sameen (INDIA) ... page 294

Nattie O'Sheggzy (NIGERIA) ... page 295
Ndue Ukaj (KOSOVO) ... page 243
Neal Whitman (USA) ... page 296
Neha Bhandarkar (INDIA) ... page 297
Nivedita Karthik (INDIA) ... page 299
Nolo Segundo (USA) ... page 300
Dr. Nurit Israeli (USA / ISRAEL) ... page 17
Onoruoiza Mark Onuchi (NIGERIA) ... page 301
Pamela Brothers Denyes (USA) ... page 302
Pankhuri Sinha (INDIA) ... page 303
Patricia Smekal (CANADA) ... page 34
Patrick O'Shea (NETHERLANDS) ... page 304
Patty Walnick (USA) ... page 305
Paul Parker (ENGLAND) ... page 306
Dr. Perwaiz Shaharyar (INDIA) ... page 200
Peter David Goodwin (USA) ... page 272
Peter W. Morris (USA) ... page 307
Ranjit Sahu (USA) ... page 311
Rebecca K. Leet (USA) ... page 308
Rebecca Lowe (WALES) ... page 92
Rebecca Sutton (NEW ZEALAND) ... page 309
Dr. Rehmat Changaizi (PAKISTAN) ... page 168
Rhonda Parsons (USA) ... page 232
Richard Spisak (USA) ... page 230
Rita B. Rose (USA) ... page 229
Rohan Facey (JAMAICA) ... page 221
Rohini Sunderam (CANADA / INDIA / BAHRAIN) ... page 226
Rose Menyon Heflin (USA) ... page 235
Roy J. Adams (CANADA) ... page 227
Rubilyn Bollion Cadao (HONG KONG / PHILIPPINES) ... page 312
Rupsingh Bhandari (NEPAL) ... page 224
Russell Willis (USA) ... page 222
S. D. Kilmer (USA) ... page 220
Sabyasachi Nazrul (BANGLADESH) ... page 75
Dr. Sajid Hussain (PAKISTAN) ... page 218
Sally Zakariya (USA) ... page 76
Sandy Phillips (ENGLAND) ... page 219
Sara Sarna (USA) ... page 216
Dr. Sarah Clarke (ENGLAND) ... page 217
Sheryl L. Fuller (USA) ... page 65
Smeetha Bhoumik (INDIA) ... page 123
Sobhna Poona (SOUTH AFRICA) ... page 310
Soo Strong (ENGLAND) ... page 213
Sreekanth Kopuri (INDIA) ... page 164
Stephen Ferrett (SCOTLAND) ... page 215
Stephen Kingsnorth (WALES / ENGLAND) ... page 102

Stephen Poole (ENGLAND) ... page 205
Suchismita Ghoshal (INDIA) ... page 147
Sudhakar Gaidhani (INDIA) ... page 162
Sunayna Pal (USA) ... page 160
Sunitha Srinivas C (INDIA) ... page 42
Susan Notar (USA) ... page 37
Susie James (USA) ... page 140
Suzan Denis (CANADA) ... page 98
Suzanne Newman (ENGLAND) ... page 161
Tamam Kahn (USA) ... page 40
Tandra Mishra (INDIA) ... page 214
Tatiana Gritsan-Chonka (UKRAINE) ... page 158
Til Kumari Sharma (NEPAL) ... page 146
Todd Matson (USA) ... page 211
Tony Daly (USA) ... page 27
Tony Frisby (ENGLAND) ... page 137
Tricia Lloyd Waller (ENGLAND) ... page 130
Trish Saunders (USA) ... page 273
Vanessa Caraveo (USA) ... page 112
Victoria Walker (ENGLAND) ... page 136
Wilda Morris (USA) ... page 233
William Khalipwina Mpina (MALAWI) ... page 93
William R. Stoddart (USA) ... page 144
Xanthi Hondrou-Hill (GREECE) ... page 210
Xavier Panadès I Blas (WALES / SPAIN) ... page 110
Xe M. Sánchez (SPAIN) ... page 152

POETRY FOR UKRAINE

Poetry in support of Ukraine,
from poets around the world.

"War is a dirty idea that grows in the heads of criminals and tyrants."
Hussein Habasch

David Webb (ENGLAND)
Based in Barnet, David holds strong views on many things. He writes both stories and poems, some of which have been published.
E: webb77@btinternet.com

24 FEBRUARY 2022

Last week, she planted seeds,
Breaking the hard ground in her yard,
Sowing the promise of summer.
Sunflowers,
Tall and strong,
Yellow against the blue.

Today a soldier comes, a boy her grandson's age.
She fixes him with her eye,
Her cracked hand full of seeds.
'What's this, babushka?'
'Put them in your pocket.
My flowers will grow where you fall.'

Tomorrow, I will plant,
In my own soft soil,
Sowing the promise of summer.
Sunflower seeds.
I take some in my hand,
To whom should I give them?

Larry Jaffe (USA)
Larry lives in Florida. He is an internationally known and acclaimed award-winning writer, author, and poet. For his entire professional career, Larry has been using his art to promote human rights.
E: larry@lgjaffe.com
W: www.lgjaffe.com
FB: larryjaffe
Twitter: @larryjaffe
Instagram: @lgjaffe

SPEAK TO ME FROM OPEN WOUNDS
Dedicated to the people of the Ukraine

Speak to me from open wounds
and how memories are lost

It is a luxury
to laugh out loud

It is a luxury
to eat bad food

It is a luxury
to still have neighbours

It is a luxury
to be able to cry

It is a luxury
to hug your children

It is not a luxury
to fight back

It is not a luxury
to still have hope

It is not a luxury
to have strong spirit

It is not a luxury
to be victorious

Kirsty Niven (SCOTLAND)
Kirsty lives and writes in Dundee. Her writing has been published in several anthologies, journals and magazines, as well as on the Web.
E: kaniven13@outlook.com
Instagram: @kanivenpoetry

I CAN'T LET IT GO

Cherubic face in Technicolor animation
with a grizzly grey background,
surrounded by sleeping bags rather than snow.
Her mouth pops open
and it should be ready to shout, to scream,
but instead she sings her heart out.

A moment frozen in time,
one I hope she gets to look back on.

James Coburn (USA)
An inductee into the Oklahoma Journalism Hall of Fame, James is also an award-winning poet whose work can be found in publications, journals and anthologies worldwide.
E: jccwriterman@gmail.com

BLACK WING PASSING

Block after block,the shutter of little feet.The silence of the dead; who will speak? Putin's propaganda war machine closes in on breath, a hospital, citizen soldiers, and row-on-row of flickering lamps.
Thirsty, exhausted, another night in Soviet-era tunnels cold and damp, scant bits of bread. A mother's despair, a campfire flame. "Is anything the same?" Gone, gone, gone.
Voices sing the dream, invisible in Putin's propaganda machine, set to feed curious Russians, reasons pointed upside down, a twisted and shivering fallout on cake sliced apart by one ageing man sitting at the edge of a table — alone, his back across the room, not to approach as he impregnates fear, aborting lives, pontificating."Give them crumbs."
Bombs away, no more play. Parasitic words of a maggot devour reason. Bodies pile horror in trenches. Cover the dead. Nearby, the blackbirds roost, fly away, away. Haze penetrates the sky. Cities burn skin.War is a massacre within the megalomaniac's eye. Smile for your camera, KGB Officer Putin in your slaughterhouseof Stalin dreams / Hitler schemes.You are their malice that won you over. You surrendered.
Who will come at this desperate hour to sing the soul of Ukraine? Oh, rise above the square and restin the tunnels of Kyiv as we sing.
Brotherhood of resistance shall not dance on puppet strings. It is the song of freedom rising not to fall again. We shall spread our voice We shall not be silent.
Mothers in Moscow will say,"Where is my son?" Dead in Putin's drum. "Where are we going?"the young Russian soldier said. No answers for the dead. Rain of fire overhead.

Dr. Nurit Israeli (USA / ISRAEL)
Born in Jerusalem, living in New York, Nurit is a psychologist who views the world through a poetic lens. She is internationally published, and has won a number of awards for her work.
E: drnurit@aol.com

HOW MUCH LONGER?

"We shall find peace. We shall hear angels.
We shall see the sky sparkling with diamonds."
~ Anton Chekov, Uncle Vania

Tell me, when shall we find peace?

When will sounds of bombs
stop thundering across
war-ravaged human habitats,
and innocent civilians will
no longer need to flee through
bullets and corpses, as their
homes become danger zones?

How much more?

It's unbearable:
The sleep of a little girl,
wearing a pink unicorn pyjamas,
interrupted mid-dream
by a shell blast on her family home,
as streets where children used
to play turn into battlefields.

It's inconceivable:
On Twitter, a man discovers
images of lifeless beloved bodies –
his wife and their two children lying
motionless on a blood-stained ground.
He recognizes their luggage.
That's how he knows.

When will it end?

Tell me, when will a sparkling
innocent sky be free of man-made
trespassers poisoning the air,
and the voice of spilled blood

will stop crying out onto us from
bodies found in charred remains
saturated with anguish?

What about all those promises,
still unkept, carried from war to war –
passed on from one generation
to the next like Olympic torches –
in lyrics of prayer-like peace songs,
sung in scores of languages
in lands tired of bloodshed?

When will hearts no longer
race in fear?

I'm still searching for answers,
and my time to patiently wait
is running out fast:
At (almost) 80, the number
that is my age is ticking forward.
I've lived through too many wars,
and it's getting late.

Yes, I'm still craving answers,
even though.
But amid wars,
only the questions live on.

Someone please tell me:
How much longer?
How much more?

David Dephy (USA / GEORGIA)
Based in New York, David is a Georgian/American award-winning poet and novelist. Named as *"A Literature Luminary"*, his poetry has won multiple prestigious awards around the world.
E: dephy21@yahoo.com

DIVINE UKRAINE

Your eyes are the eyes of God.
Your breath is mother tongue of Earth.
Your blood is a symphony of fire.
Your lips are the truth-tellers,
no one can take your golden mystery,
no one can feel you without admiration.
Your heart is garden of kisses.
Your ears are pearls of expectation.
Your words are constellations –
the faces of heroes, encircled by rays,
drifted on the minds of the world,
their smile, their look, their strength and its innocence,
a tide that tugs at us. In times like these,
a sense washes over us, and we gather together
in the deadly noise of millennium and this stillness,
a stillness that never wavers.
All we have become, divine Ukraine,
is what your innocence has made of us.
The naked homeland of freedom
beats right in your heart.

Hussein Habasch (KURDISTAN)
Hussein is a poet from Afrin. He has published 12 books, his poems has been translated into over 20 languages, and he has work published in a large number of international anthologies.
E: habasch70@hotmail.com
FB: @hussein.habasch

THE WAR!

War weaves its grudges from terrifying faces
War sends gifts of death to all sides of love.

Suddenly, the resurrection sets in with open mouth like hell
Suddenly, children's skulls are flying in the air
Suddenly, the heart of life is extinguished.

War passes its yellow roar from the mouth of predatory engines.
War usurps the earth and the sky.

In the war
Suddenly the blood flows profusely
Suddenly the bodies burn
Suddenly the lungs crack
Suddenly the creatures die

War is unbearable cruelty
War is ruins
War is disgusting arrogance
War is debauchery
War is blindness ...

War ...
War ...
War ...
War is a dirty idea that grows in the heads of criminals and tyrants.

Geoffrey Heptonstall (ENGLAND)
Based in Cambridge, Geoffrey is a poet, writer, and playwright. He taught creative writing at university, and several of his plays have been produced for London fringe theatres.
E: geoffreylit@gmail.com

THE PROMISE

Dust blows in the dry winds,
darkening the lately fallen snow.
Brick and glass are scattered
as symbols of survival
when a plague of fire fell
in a cold winter war.
Torn flesh and raw bone are thrown
into the makeshift tombs,
One day there must be a memorial.
The living have vanished so soon.
Hope of return is left behind,
but life shall find its way again
when the enemy is silenced
by the peace that remains the promise.

Cathy Cade (ENGLAND)
Cathy is a retired librarian based in Cambridgeshire. Her writing has been published in a number of magazines and anthologies worldwide.
W: www.cathy-cade.com

UNDERGROUND

Above us, bombs fall all around.
Our homeland crumbles into dust
and families huddle underground.

Trapped here in holes, like vermin found
crouched under rocks, meanwhile we must
listen to bombs fall all around.

Missiles fly and mortars pound
our lives to rubble. So unjust,
while we must huddle underground.

Above, our homes come tumbling down,
victims of a madman's lust
for power; bombs falling all around.

Down here, as sobs and whimpers sound,
our hopes are crumbling into dust
while families huddle underground.

And more explosions shake the ground,
and debris rains, and backwinds gust,
and bombs are falling all around
while families huddle underground.

James Aitchison (AUSTRALIA)
James is an author and poet who lives in an old goldfields town. His poems have been included in Australian anthologies, and many other poetry magazines.
E: jimbooks@hotmail.com

ONCE UPON A TIME IN UKRAINE

Once upon a time in Ukraine,
did they have music?
Did people dance and hold hands?
Once upon a time in Ukraine,
were babies born on quiet mornings?
Were they baptised in glorious old churches?
Once upon a time in Ukraine,
did people walk in parks?
Were flowers blooming?
Once upon a time in Ukraine,
did children play at school and sing?
Did young women tend to their beauty?
Once upon a time in Ukraine,
did farmers cherish wheatfields?
Did the wide blue sky bless their efforts?
Once upon a time in Ukraine …

Jack Henry (USA)
Jack is a writer based in California. Any acknowledgement of accomplishments feels petty as the people of Ukraine suffer with the war crimes committed against them by Russia.
E: jackhenry951@hotmail.com

BY DAWN'S EARLY LIGHT

as the multi-million-dollar yachts
of oligarchs
sit at anchor,
impounded by an
enraged world,
i wonder how
the embattled citizens
of Mariupol
will find their next meal.

i wonder how
leaders of free and
so-called democratic countries
sleep at night,
i wonder how
CEOs in a petrochemical
industry justify their millions,
i wonder how
women and children,
refugees of injustice,
sleep in the quiet
of asylum,

i wonder if anything
will change
after the button
is pushed
and the world turns
to ash.

Jasna Šamić (FRANCE / BOSNIA & HERZEGOVINA)
Born in Sarajevo, living in Paris, Jasna is the author of a number of books, and is a lecturer of Balkan languages, literature, history and civilizations.
E: samicjasna@gmail.com

UKRAINE

The sirens that howl at night in the cities
From the invaded country
Can they be compared to hyenas,
And the poison to arrow missiles?

Can the Bear invade the dreams of the attacked country?

No sirens in the City of Light
But its nights are shaken by giant spears
No Bear either in the country where our
Dreams howl like hyenas

Terror threatens our stunted spring and
Poison arrows - our broken hearts

While the oceans tremble with the song of
Persephone while Ares threatens with
Hades
Where a wily Cerberus with many missile heads
Barks from its thousand demented mouths

Beckham Lim (SINGAPORE)
Beckham is a 15 year-old secondary school student. He has been able to consecutively achieve a first for two years running at his school's poetry slam.
E: beckham.1.lim.1@gmail.com
Instagram: @beckhams_poetry

THE SUNFLOWER

I stand tall in a field of gold, swaying with the wind
A distant peel of thunder, heralds the arrival of beating hearts
A young man, rifle in hand, pushes past my brothers and sisters
Torch in the other, he sets them ablaze
The smoke that hazes the skies choke me, as it lays waste to my beloved land
Ash, like fire flies fly free on this barren land, sorrowful and grey
The thick blood, velvet red, pours down on me
Into the dark soil, it seeps down deep
Like a river it flows, endless
Through the scorching land and winding streams, I stand tall
A flock of steel birds screech overhead, as a hail of lead follows
The withered land scarred by time, with craters and holes scattered on the ashen path
The constant banging and flashing light scares me to the core
As noon reaches I look up, whispering my goodbyes
A cloud of dust and dirt covers me, laying me to rest
Oh, sunflower who stood tall, may you rest well
As the land you once stood in, it gives you its dearest farewell

Tony Daly (USA)
Tony is a creative writer based in the Washington DC Metro A
is a retired veteran of the U.S. Air Force Reserves, and volunteers as
an Associate Editor for a military and arts magazine.
E: Aldaly13@gmail.com
W: www.aldaly13.wixsite.com/website
Twitter: @aldaly18

HOLD THE LINE

Knowing death is upon you,
yet struggling for every breathe,
for every measure of existence.
For every hour
is another hour
for another to escape.

Hearing Valkyries cry
from winged steads' metallic backs,
while holding your position,
shielding hospitals,
shielding places of faith,
shielding homes.

Struggle on,
for the world hears you.
We shall hold you up
when you haven't strength
to stand
to raise your shield -
once your spirit of battle
strides beyond this mortal realm,
communities of the world
shall embrace those
you held to protect.

Carol Parris Krauss (USA)
Carol is a mother, teacher, and poet from Virginia. She enjoys using place/nature as theme vehicles, and has won a number of awards for her poetry.
W: www.carolparriskrausspoet.com
FB: @CarolPKrauss
Twitter: @CarolKrauss3

THE FLOWERS WILL GROW, BASK IN THE SUN

It's a sad excuse for a sunflower, Spindly, pale green.
Only one from a dozen seeds. No flower to speak of.
Every year, the same results. I buy the best seeds, use
the richest soil. Call them baby, and gift them time under

fluorescent lights. The transfer to the front yard, a ritual
conducted with military precision. Then failure. No blooms
to dance on the wind, relish spring rains on their upturned faces.
Voles wait and watch. Burrow under them, wreck their roots,

turn the soil away from their thin stems. And yet, I persist.
Long for a bed full of sunflowers. And I know, without fail,
they will one day grow strong, build sturdy roots, and fend
off the rodents to stand tall. Bask in the sun.

Eduard Schmidt-Zorner (REPUBLIC OF IRELAND)
Eduard is a translator and writer of poetry, haibun, haiku and stories. He has published in over 160 international anthologies, literary journals and broadsheets.
E: EadbhardMcGowan@gmx.com

FORGE PEACE

They still wait
for the right time to sow,
ploughshares stand ready,
to divide the soil into furrows,
even and parallel,
they face dark times,
indecisive, hesitant, idle,
as steel storms rage
not far away.

Is it worthwhile
to till the field,
to tend the land,
plan for a yield,
as on the wide horizon
gunfire and bombs
light up the nights?

The cannons bark,
the tank tracks rattle,
shelling on cities.
The will to plant the seeds
and hope for a rich harvest
sinks.

People will die on the fields,
the soil their grave,
their blood will fertilise
the humus,
the plough remains
in the shed, unused,
a horse scrapes the floor in the barn,
the full seed basket,
gives the birds a big feed,
ploughshares became swords
again
instead to forge the swords
for good
into a peaceful tool.

Amelia Fielden (AUSTRALIA)
Amelia is a writer, poet and translator, based in Wollongong. She is fluent in Japanese, and has spent much of her life engrossed in its culture.
E: anafielden@gmail.com

UNTITLED

destroyed
by Russian bombardment
a hospital
for women, children, babes -
my useless fury of tears

Caroline Johnson (USA)
Based near Chicago, former newspaper journalist and English teacher, Caroline has has published internationally and won numerous state and national poetry awards.
W: www.caroline-johnson.com
FB: @carolinejohnsonauthor
Instagram: @caroline.johnson.585555
Twitter: @twinkscat

GLASS OF SADNESS

Tinted, shimmering sadness
grandma's cup of gladness
                striking targets, convoy in Kiev
family heirloom, now
with jagged edges
                multi-rocket launcher
my mother born in flight
from Nazis, Grandma saved
these tiny, tiny glasses
                smoke billowing
my daughter looks like her,
used to drink from the cup
                sanctions sanctions sanctions

Ukraine, this glass is stained
won't ever be the same
                citizens sleep in subways
                to avoid air strikes
can you see the mirrored
eye, my tears falling.

Joseph A. Farina (CANADA)
Joseph lives in Ontario. He is a retired lawyer and award winning poet. He has published two books of poetry, and his work can be seen in literary journals and magazines across North America.
E: jfarina@cogeco.ca

УКРАЇНА

blue and gold tint our eyes
in fields in cities everywhere
colours of defiance and courage
against the colossus of war
we witness freedom's call
in blue air and golden sunlight
against the shadowed tyranny
her children gathering in survival
to face the rising iron storm
that would darken their skies
and blot out their sun forever

Janelyn Dupingay Vergara (SINGAPORE / PHILIPPINES)
Janelyn has worked as a domestic worker in Singapore since 2015. She is a core team member with the Migrant Writers of Singapore, and one of the featured speakers at the Singapore Writers Festival.
E: janelynvergara24.jv@gmail.com
FB: @Jane Lyn Dupingay
Instagram: @jane25_lyn

WHEN FURY FINDS NO HALT

Under the same sky
Sharing sunlight and raindrops
Inhaling the same air,
Welcoming night and day
Yet, remained strangers
Throwing curses.
Anger reaches insanity,
Humanity has gone to its rest
While the world pleads
For reincarnation of peace
But will remain a dream
While fire never stops
Burning healthy bushes
Turning them to ashes.
Only left is a voice
Begging to spare
A moment of breath
But none listens,
Deafened by the roaring outrage
And satisfaction lies
In seeing body falling.
Sigh for the earth's surface
That witness the
Indomitable brutality of a man.

Patricia Smekal (CANADA)
Patricia lives by the sea on Vancouver Island. Her poetry has been winning prizes since 2003, and has appeared in over 70 print publications, in Canada and abroad.
E: jazzsmekal@shaw.ca

UKRAINE

Ukraine,
you cry
for those
whose lives
are shattered
by an unjust war—
terror and destruction
flung from ruptured skies.

Ukraine,
you cry,
we weep
as tears are torn
from freedom's eyes.

Ukraine,
you grieve,
as well you know
the cost of peace—
yet survival seems to
rise from rubbled streets.

Ukraine,
we acclaim
your courage!
Such determination
strengthens our beliefs
that tyranny cannot thrive
and democracy will never die.

Dr. Lynne Sedgmore CBE (ENGLAND)
Lynne lives in Glastonbury. She is a poet, priestess, coach and leadership developer, and has published three collections of poetry. She was awarded the CBE in 2004 for services to education.
E: lynne.sedgmore@gmail.com
W: www.lynnesedgmore.co.uk
Linkedin: @dr-lynne-sedgmore-cbe-b10553211

CHILDREN OF UKRAINE

Diana holds her cuddly bear to comfort her.
Andriy stands frozen - no toy to hold.
His bear abandoned in the siren screeching rush
for safety, and a huddled basement space.

Mariya sees the bomb that kills her mum
right before her eyes, they close too late.
Always she will see the horror of this sight,
Over and over and over again.

In a dark bleak shelter another child is born,
her face a rainbow, shining rays of innocence.
Precious new life brings a momentary joy -
fading fast in tomorrow's bombs.

No father's hand to hold in the dark of war,
Always walking, queuing, waiting, watching.
Fear and terror mingling with stories of hope
and the welcome kindness of strangers.

Trauma and destruction everywhere,
Outside, inside and within.
Bodies, minds and buildings damaged.
Too many beyond repair.

Millions fleeing, displaced, distraught and terrified.
No child deserves to fear their death through war.
Ninety children already dead.
Hundreds more may die.

Igor draws bombs and tanks and guns - pauses -
Writes "peace and victory" large upon the page.
Smiling as he shows his grandmother,
His wise child knowing "we will win" through
Ukrainian courage, heroism, unity and national pride.

Eliza Segiet (POLAND)
Multi award-winning writer and poet, Eliza's work can be found in anthologies, books and literary magazines worldwide.
E: eliza.anna@op.pl

PROCESSION
Translated by Artur Komoter

In the rotten basement,
the never-ending silence
allows
to reflect
on the time
that has mocked people.

No one
was prepared
for total evil.

Nobody expected
that
it could have nowhere
to escape to.

No one knew
that the procession of life
would end against our will
☐ the procession of death
in mass graves.

Susan Notar (USA)
Based in Virginia, Susan has worked helping vulnerable communities in the Middle East, and currently works at the U.S. State Department. Her poetry has appeared in a number of international publications.
E: susananotar@gmail.com

KYIV 2022

In 1995 after the fall of the Great Bear
I arrived with a Ukrainian dictionary and in snow boots
looking forward to borscht and chicken Kiev
meetings with new women leaders.

Border guards still wore Russian uniforms
street signs spoke Russian
restaurants gave me menus
and had nothing listed on them
exhausted unsmiling waitresses
presented me with processed meat and vodka instead.
At one alleged meeting in an apartment building
seemingly the crumbling set for *Doctor Zhivago*
a snarling dog lunged
to save me a neighbour threw it a hunk of bloody beef.

Still. Hope scented the cold air.

Today a forty-mile convoy of Russian trucks stalls
en route to Kyiv.
the young conscripts inside barely able to grow beards.
Ukrainians blow up bridges
make Molotov cocktails at breweries
retirees train on AK-47s.
Expectant mothers cower in basement bunkers
too laden with child to flee for Poland or Moldova.

Here, we witness
    send food
    dedicate music
    write poems

to the people who have tasted freedom.

Craven L. Sutton, Jr (USA)
Craven lives in North Carolina. Since his retirement, he has written more than 500 poems, primarily in four collections, reflecting an affinity for musicality in poetry.
E: cravensutton@gmail.com

MY UKRAINE

Faithful Father, hear my plea,
True to Thee, our hearts remain,
Now, with peace and liberty,
Bless my homeland of Ukraine.

From Crimea, to the highland,
From the mountains to the sea,
On the plains, forever my land,
We shall live, forever, free!

O'er the fields of golden grain,
Beauty, every eye can see,
Voice of freedom, sing again,
With the joy of liberty!

Smoke clouds darken, now, the sky,
And the tyrant's voice I hear,
As the valiant bleed and die,
For this land, we hold so dear!

Every soldier is my brother,
And his keeper I shall be,
All his burdens, I will shoulder,
As we fight for liberty!

On the shores, along the Dnieper,
Every heart shall beat as one,
Hand in hand, we'll stand together,
Till our victory is won!

Hear the music of Lysenko,
Beauty in Shevchenko's songs,
In our hearts, their voices echo,
With their spirit, we are strong!

Soon, there'll be no sounds of war,
Liberty and peace shall reign,
We shall sing, for evermore,
Freedom lives, in my Ukraine!

Carol Moeke (ENGLAND)
Carol lives in London. Since retiring from teaching, she's put her mind to writing, and has had work published in a number of magazines.
E: carolmoeke@hotmail.com

THE UNOPENED GIFT

I received the gift of peace today
but I didn't open it.
I found it hard to hold it
in hands not making prayerful thanks.
They can't, I can't, there's anger.
Anger at ineptitude,
anger at loud silence,
anger at great posturing,
and absence of solution.
Anger at what I don't know,
anger at what I do know,
and pain, my pain not good enough
to help, or even comfort
those poor folk, the innocents
in the hands of the Herod in our midst.

Tamam Kahn (USA)
Based in California, Tamam spent two decades researching early Islamic history and is the author two award-winning books on the women of early Islam.
E: tamam@completeword.com
W: www.completeword.wordpress.com

MARIUPOL — AFTER THE BLAST

I wake to a great explosion,
alone—on the tenth floor.

shattered window glass, fright.
No water, heat or phone. Cold rushes in.

The blast shuts out the sun.
Overcoat over my pyjamas. Running.

Running from my home in old slippers—
Over. Across. Down the broken stairway

Urgent voices. Shouts and cries.
No one's waiting for anybody.

Outside in smoke and snow
I am holding my keys, where to?

A close explosion shakes the sidewalk.
I fall to the ground and cover my head.

I scratch at the snow for words.
Icy cold wind is the reply.

Apartment and car keys still in my hand,
my hand clutched in blood,

My ears ringing in a phantom world.
I don't remember where I am.

I draw a blank, taste adrenaline.
Someone is lifting me. I'm alive.

What's next?

Eric Forsbergh (USA)
Based in Virginia, Eric is a Vietnam veteran of the Navy, and a retired dentist. He has won the Poetry Society of Virginia's Edgar Allen Poe Memorial (2013 & 2014), and has been published internationally.
E: forsber@verizon.net

A WEAPONS LIST FOR KYIV

Today I fund a weapons list.
In this crisis
not another dime just now
for elephants or whales.
Not for migratory birds.
Not for ocean cleanup.
Not bats. Not bees.

I see a man confront a tank
with just himself.
Him pushing back seems almost comic,
then he kneels.
In another battered town,
two parents and a child sprawl,
covered with a tarp,
the father's hand protruding toward
an upright, untouched suitcase.
Meters beneath the rubble of her high-rise
a woman births her baby
between two flashlit subway tracks.

A torn edge of fabric
juts up from a Molotov.
The ripping sound
of missiles can be heard on video.
Ragged moments gape
between the last breath
and the absence of the next.
An arcing shell rends
a church's golden dome.

Today I fund a weapons list.
Next, I'll crowdsource mobile kitchens,
clothing drives, formula and diapers,
warm shelters, and blankets
for refugees who carry their children
and the weightless ashes of their freedoms.

Sunitha Srinivas C (INDIA)
Sunitha works as an associate professor at a government college in Kerala. She has published a number of books and poems with international publishers.
E: sunita.srinivas@gmail.com
FB: @suni.srini
Instagram:@sunitha_srinivas_c

AN UNFOLDING ATTACK

Pain
    of the displaced
    of the homeless
Loss
    of friends
    of family
    of a home
    of life
unfolds
Memories beautiful that haunt forever

Assault by land and sea
Airstrikes, hostages, curfews
The fear, the escape, the hope
The past and future
As troops and tanks, missiles and bombs
Shred the air and declare evacuation

A military occupation unfolding
Before a world buzzing with Live Updates

Troops pour across borders
Missiles rain
Drones fly
Smoke spirals and chokes
Gunfire rattles and scars
Sirens blare and pierce

Gridlocked metros and subways
Exhausted sleeping bags
Fatigued bomb shelters refuge
People stranded

Fuelled unrest
Tensions escalate
Civilians flee

A regime dismantled
An economy derailed
A crisis declared

Back in an age of confrontation
Needless acts of aggression
Shocking violence and fierce resistance
Collective responses that condemn
An invasion launched

A world explodes before me
Leaving lives shrouded in dust

Defuse
Stop your troops
Stop your assault
Stop your televised menacing speeches
YOU will be accountable
For all the blood that is shed

Alex Hand (AUSTRALIA)
Alex is a poet, essayist, short story writer and editor from Queensland. He draws inspiration for his work from many sources including community, civic society and a caring pace of life.
W: www.alex-hand.com
Instagram: @aleksander.hand

REALITY IS NOT A PLAY THING

In *Alice Through the Looking Glass* reality is conceivably up for grabs
equally maybe in some argumentative post-modern posturing.
But in the concrete world, where rain is wet and falls from above,
the oceans ebb and flow, in and out, without question or quibble,
here, in existence, we accept by common agreement what is fact.
For example, the painting of the Sistine Chapel is quite incredible
or that wallabies and platypi are distinctly antipodean animals
and that government by the people is unconditionally sovereign;
these things modern humans, thinking people, take as actuality.

Unlike an unfinished script on the page, reality is not a play thing,
nor by contrast with wet clay on a potter's wheel, is it mouldable
by the aspirations of any new Caesar in very lightly padded cells.
Immigration officials stamping passports show where the border is,
archives from parliament record the civic evolution of homelands,
Putin, et al, reality is not a play thing, Ukraine is not a play thing.

Jonathan Ukah (ENGLAND / NIGERIA)
Jonathan is a graduate of English from the University of Nigeria. He studied Law in Germany, but lives and writes in London.
E: johnking1502@gmail.com

WHEN YOU FIGHT FOR YOUR COUNTRY

And when you fight for your country,
Fight with the nerve of a new empire,
Where elephants stand and stare
As birds of beauty peck up victory
With songs that wake the stones;
Fight where trees line up as flowers
And sunflowers swing in the wind,
Reaching out to blend with the blue sky;
Fight where woods stand like ordered soldiers,
Four-leafed clovers littering the pavements,
Where the bright blue sky hush down
The lanes of manicured fields of yellow;
When you decide to fight for your country,
A crown of glory awaits your triumph
Like a golden box of Turkish delight,
A wreath of heroism, of incredible honour
Floating on the air of wild celebration,
Shall greet the surge of a new kingdom.
There shall be a rain of blue and green,
Where red splashes on the wall like spilt paint,
Where you build an empire of yellow stones,
Born of nerves and marks, you left behind,
Marks of your love, marks of victory.
When indeed you fight for your country,
Even crumpled flowers on the hill
Shall stir up and sing for you.

Lynn White (WALES)
Based in north Wales, Lynn's work is influenced by issues of social justice and events, places and people she has known or imagined.
W: www.lynnwhitepoetry.blogspot.com
FB: @Lynn-White-Poetry

WHERE ARE THEY NOW

In 1967 I hitch-hiked to Belgrade.
My friend and I would take an overnight train
to stay with our Albanian friends
in what is now Kosovo.
Until then we had some hours to kill.

The local cafe culture called
and we ate a modest meal,
two great slabs
of the ubiquitous cheese puff pastry
washed down with colas.

We went to the counter to pay
but the Server refused our money.
He pointed to a table where some guys
were enjoying a few beers.
They had already paid, he said.

We were mystified.
They had made no contact with us
and we tried to tell them we could not accept.
They explained that
they wished to thank us
for the help Britain had given in WW2.

Fast forward to 1999
when the right to self determination was all the rage.
and NATO bombs were falling on Belgrade.
I thought about them a lot back then.
I think of them now
when the bombs
fall in Europe
once again.

And I still have my friend in Kosovo.
Sometimes we feel human,
sometimes not.

David Sparenberg (USA)
Based in the Pacific Northwest, David is an internationally published author, essayist and eco-poet.
E: earthartsturtleisland@yahoo.com

EUCHARIST OF WAR

Eat this.
There is not
much time for eating. We
fight and
food is scarce and
getting scarcer.

Maybe this is
our last supper? Perhaps
the world is ending?

This shattered bone-bread
is bodies of our people –
fallen, falling
bread crumbs and
scattered black seeds of sunflowers.

Citizens who are
dismembered sleep now, never
to waken again, cold, voiceless
in the wet snow of war. Dazed
confused, forlorn lovers, lonely
and afraid
seek one another. Search
where the sky is collapsed.

One
perhaps an orphaned child in
a heavy, winter coat
or maybe a homeless cripple
trudges away. Where do the
old and the sick go to hide?

Drink this.
Who knows if
and when we might drink again?
Press your lips with us to
the breath and tear-stained cup
and taste the bittersweet of

what it takes for
some human beings to
be allowed to be human.
Humans ...

This is the blood
of our people – spilling, lamenting
along bombed out
streets, blown building and
the fields where
once sunflowers grew. Tall
golden witnesses to bygone peace.

We are dying in Ukraine
for freedom.
The whole world is watching.
We are dying.

Chrys Salt MBE (ENGLAND / SCOTLAND)
Based between London and Edinburgh, Chrys is a performer and widely published and anthologized poet. She has performed in festivals across the world, and written in almost every genre.
E: chrys@chryssalt.com
W: www.chryssalt.com
W: www.biglit.org

MISSING

As soon as he could walk
he'd abseil down the cot side –
pad in low-slung pyjamas
down the corridor to hide.
She'd hunt and call - alarmed
at first - then it became a nightly ritual,
a game, with him unharmed,
chuckling his guttural
chuckle when she found
him in his wicker toy-basket
gone to ground
with soldier, tank and rabbit -
or holed up in his duvet –
keeping cave with Marmite
baited breath – primed to waylay
her with bombardments of delight.

Now she can't find him anywhere.
Her care unplugged, the ariel
of her sixth sense 'off air.'
He's lost, gone AWOL
from her mothering radar.
She scans photographs, unpicks
the tabloid propaganda –
the multi-media rhetoric -
fillets the news analysis
for clues. Prays for a sighting
of him on a dusty road, his
Battery delivering aid - not fighting!
She magnifies the map.
The names of foreign town and street
are anagrams she can't unwrap
his camouflage – complete.

Martyn Hesford (ENGLAND)
Based in Scarborough. Martyn is a BAFTA nominated, award-winning writer, best-known for his feature film about artist L.S. Lowry, starring Vanessa Redgrave and Timothy Spall.
E: martynhesford@btopenworld.com
Amazon: Martyn-Hesford/e/B092W4PF92

DO YOU SCREAM

do you scream.
do they watch you
the soldiers

like an insect
in a glass box
trapped.

all their
feelings
gone.
switched off.

are you muffled.
gagged.

your mouth is open wide
a hole.

do you scream.

do you slowly
slowly fade away
knowing
you
are nothing
to them.

do they rub you
away
knowing
you are the same

redness of blood
their stain.

do they

will they

ever feel again.
see.

in the fields

still.
a wild poppy
grows.

Kelly Madden (CANADA)
Kelly lives in British Columbia. Her work has appeared in a number of anthologies and publications, and her first collection of poetry has just been released.
E: raspjam2002@hotmail.com
W: www.kellybmadden.com

CRUSH

Hopelessness came to me like a sickness
when I saw the evil that befell
your streets, your fields, your homes

despair pushed into me
in hearing your pleas
for the world to help you

at times I wanted to lie flat, in a field
such was the crush of sadness for you all
but I still stand; I will not crush the small flowers

I still stand, and am praying for Ukraine every day
I still stand, and beg the Gods to extinguish your pain
I still stand, and am sending my love to Ukraine

Glory to the people of Ukraine
Glory to the animals and plants and insects of Ukraine
Glory to the ancient, fertile lands and green hills of Ukraine
Glory to the light that always wins over darkness

Glory to Ukraine!

Jocelyn Boor (USA)
Jocelyn lives in Milwaukee and teaches art history. She writes and composes poetry whenever a marking implement finds her hand, and has had a few poems published.
E: jocelyn@eldamar.net

RESILIENCE

I cannot write a poem for Ukraine.
My family has seen too many wars
Grandfathers (WWI)
Father and uncles (WWII, Korea)
Cousins (Viet Nam, Iraq, Afghanistan)
But we did not talk about these or
How utterly unnecessary these wars were.

I watched wars unfold on TV
And now, the Internet
I am barraged not by missiles
But by continuing images of
Bombed out buildings
Dying children
Cities, towns, villages in ruins

This war feels different,
Unprovoked, unwanted.
Complete destruction is the goal.
But I am invigorated by tractors stealing tanks
A little girl singing in a bomb shelter
And beer bottles transforming into lethal cocktails
And the overwhelming resolve my grandfathers would recognize.
Ukrainian resilience is irresistible.

Carole Stone (USA)
Based in New Jersey, Carole is Distinguished Professor of English, emerita, Montclair State University. She has published a number of poetry books, and is currently working on a manuscript.
E: stonec@mail.montclair.edu

INVASION

The suffering of a people
who leave behind their jewel boxes,
their candlesticks.

Carry photos of grandparents
to fold family into sleep,
hearts with those left

in the embers of their cities.
Even with the barbarous
invasion of their country,

even while ploughing
the deep furrow of grief,
they breathe in

a sunny February morning
that can't heal
the maimed world.

At night, stars spread
like the pebbles, piled up
on the shore of the Black Sea.

Annie Wright (SCOTLAND)
Annie is an English poet living in south west Scotland. She has published two collections of poetry, runs poetry writing workshops, and helps organise the LitFlix and Big Lit festivals.
E: annie.wright01@googlemail.com

MARIUPOL
(14th March 2022)

It went viral – film of two people rescuing
a heavily pregnant woman on a stretcher
from the bombed-out maternity hospital.

She was alive, injured, but alive.
For days I prayed, hoping that she
and her baby were somehow safe.

Today came news no-one wants
to hear – blood on the stretcher was
from labour, but also a detached hip.

An emergency Caesarean within minutes
of rescue couldn't save her baby, dead
in the womb and she knew
            she knew

her chick would never fly, screaming
kill me now!   as they fought to save her
but the light had already fled her eyes.

Swallows and chicks in tens of thousands
flock to leave Ukraine, migrating to Poland
or any European nation they'll be safe.

In Mariupol there is no safe corridor.
No-one knows how many are dying
for want of water, food or basic medicine.

Without electricity mobile phones can't
chirp or tweet, untreated wounds turn
to sepsis
        there are no words for this.

Alfredo Quarto (USA)
Alfredo is an environmental activist and poet living on an organic farm in the foothills of the Olympic Mountains in Washington. He's been published in numerous poetry publications around the world.
E: mapexecdir@gmail.com

FOR THE BRAVE WOMEN OF KYIV

She leaned against the wall
holding her assault rifle loosely
in both hands the barrel pointing
to ground her nails still polished
red and her fingers slender meant
to caress a lover or smooth a fold
of dress or hold a child's hand
not meant to grip the pain
of Putin's bloody war.

Her transport truck would soon
depart to take her and the others
to imagined lines drawn on Kyiv's outskirts
that they are expected to hold and defend
against an enemy that has no right to be there
following orders that should never have been given
        nor should never be obeyed.

She tried to hold back her tears
as she talked to the reporter
shifting the rifle now cradled in her arms
like a dozing dangerous child
not yet ready to awake from dreams
while there's still time for sleep.

When asked if she knew how to use her weapon
she nervously laughed then gently
cried, "No, not really!"
She then paused to wipe away tears
that slid down her face in wavering lines
meant to mend her memories of loss
sewn to stitch the wounds
with her own torn threads.
"We were taught two days ago
how to use the rifle."

There is such tragic irony in war.
The AK-47 that she held is known

as the "weapon of the century"
designed and crafted by the same enemy
she must soon face on the embattled streets.
Was this really the perfect weapon
to stop the tanks, down the missiles
and halt the massing convoys and troops
closing in on her city to take away
her freedom, silence her brave president
and quell the dreams of the people of Ukraine?

As she tightened her grip around
the polished barrel of her rifle
and felt the balance of its smooth stock
pressed against her hands becoming more
familiar with their potential for defence
in this war that she never wanted
whose end unknown should come to pass
she braced herself for the battle ahead
for this was her time
there would be no other.

Eleni Vasiliou-Asteroskoni (GERMANY/GREECE)
Originally from Crete, but now based in Germany, Eleni is a Hellenic self-taught painter and poet. She has published two collections of poetry, a play, and a trilogy of children's illustrated books.
E: eleni-vasiliou@hotmail.com
W: www.asteroskoni.wordpress.com
FB: @Ελένη Βασιλείου-Αστερόσκονη
Instagram: @e.v.asteroskoni

DREAM

From afar they come I feel them,
so close, their breath
They know what needs to be done
Their ragged black wings
open to block my sun-

Like giant balls of fore
that illuminate the sky
I hear the cry of a baby
this eternal cry
of a baby who never grew up.
They came in and sowed fear everywhere
to encircle,
and shield in the darkness the light
My heart cracked asking God to intervene-
but deep down I know very well ...
How people make the same mistakes again
in a story that slept in oblivion
I smell, in the atmosphere of decay
whoever can close his eyes
the dream tonight let him sleep gently ...

Joan McNerney (USA)
Joan lives in New York. Her poetry is found in literary magazines, journals and anthologies worldwide.
E: poetryjoan@statetel.com

FLOWERS FOR THE DEAD

This is the way
I see your face.
O you are dead
your face frozen
and moist.
I miss you and search
for you everywhere as
light dims to darkness
and darkness brightens
to light.

Your days were arranged
in that small vase of time
given to you. I see your
face reflected there now.
In a vase full of
flowers for the dead,
reeds of tears.

O your face facing me.
Until my vase of time
spills over and we meet
in that season called
eternity.

Arbër Selmani (KOSOVO)
Arbër is a journalist and poet from Pristina. He has published three books, his work has been translated into eight languages, and he has participated in a number of international literature festivals.
FB: @arberselmani8
Instagram: @arberiu
Twitter: @arberiani

KIRILL WAS KILLED

Who rifts the intestines of an 18-month-old baby?
Who does that?

Who cares about the infant
of whom
we willingly signed the treaty of death?

Who?

Does more smoke come out of a building in ruins?
Or of an insane Putin?
Or, s**t out of one single man?
Or
is it from a baby who just let out the last cry today?

Who will a mother want to strangle now?
How does a dad stand on his feet?
Kirill was killed.

Who counts how many drops of blood were squeezed from a small head
of a baby?

Who?
What mechanism?

Who clears the vomit of children under bombardments?

In Ukraine, Kirill was killed today, Kirill is killed...
... so that war, oil, Kremlin, nuclear workers continue on living
... so that bloody Ukrainians with slit heads call for help.

Is it smiling, if God exists, that villain hand touched by a Russian mother?
... the hand that killed a child, a life wrapped in a war sheet

... Russian hands, Russian hands killed Kirill, are killing foetuses.

In Ukraine, Kirill is now underground ...
... the world doesn't care for a child less
... you, unfortunate baby.

Ann Privateer (USA)
Based in California, Ann is a poet, artist and photographer, and has had her work published in magazines worldwide.
E: annprivateer@gmail.com

SEPARATING

Families we see
On TV, a horror
Lost and alone
A mystery of why
No music only
Consternation
Waiting for
A new day.

Kavita Ezekiel Mendonca (CANADA / INDIA)
Based in Calgary, Kavita is of Indian origin. She has taught English, French and Spanish in various colleges and schools, both in India and overseas. Her poems have been featured in several anthologies.
E: amendonca@gmail.com
W: www.kavitaezekielpoetry.com

REMOVE WAR FROM THE DICTIONARY

I remember being seventeen, a young college girl
War broke out between my country
and a neighbouring one
The instructions were strict
Windows must be darkened with black paper
No light to show through at nights
A volunteer beat his stick loudly
"Turn off the Lights! Turn off the Lights!"
He shouted like a town crier
He had no good news.

My father was somewhere in the darkness
Fighting a battle of his own
So we clung to our mother tightly
Like koalas to eucalyptus trees
Till she couldn't breathe,
The fighter jets roared the skies
if there were bombs we prayed
They would spare the city
Fall into the sea so close to home.

I prayed for the fish
The sea is their home
I prayed for the waves
Not to burn up,
We were spared
Our home stayed standing
Some are not so lucky.

They say 'all's fair in love and war'
So far from the truth.

This war that now rages
Will stop only when
We remove the word 'war'
From our dictionaries
Keep the word, 'Peace'.

Judy Jones Brickner (USA)
Judy lives in Wisconsin. She has found that the pandemic has provided the luxury of having all the time in the world to write poetry. Her poetry has been published in a couple of local magazines.
E: jlbrickn@wisc.edu

SEEDS OF DEFIANCE

The elderly woman on *TikTok* stopped my heart
confronting a Russian soldier like a gamecock.
She didn't balk.

With a great deal of mock she shouted
"You came uninvited as an intruder, the enemy,"
There was no pleasantry.

She held out seeds for his pocket,
"These sunflowers will grow out of your eye sockets
when you are killed and die on Ukrainian soil."

Those strong yellow flowers are now a symbol of courage.
She unmasked the people's incredible defiance
fighting a giant.

Sheryl L. Fuller (USA)
Sheryl is a writer, singer songwriter, and performing artist based in Illinois. Her writing is inspired from her many life experiences, and she has had a number of books published.
E: playnickids@comcast.net

PARTY 'TIL THE BOMBS DROP

Daddy I don't want to flee,
Daddy will you think of me,
Daddy, I will be thinking of you,
I'm on the run and it's all I can do.

I don't want to leave you behind,
Please always know you are on my mind,
Oh Daddy, please make it stop,
He said, "Dance little one, and party 'til the bombs drop."

I'm longing for home in a room filled with others,
Babies and children alone with their mothers,
I head for the boarder to a land "I don't know,
Mama says hold my hand, it's time to go."

Ukraine I turn back for one last look,
Then through the gate with my passport book,
We take a bridge of tears to nowhere,
Look Mama, there's a teddy bear.

I don't want to go on, I want to go home,
I have my teddy; he too is alone,
He listens to all my hopes and dreams,
My whispers drowned out with distracting screams.

Daddy, think of me, I am thinking of you,
I'm scared for the mission you need to do,
Scared I may never see you again,
But I'm still looking forward to then.

Like a sunflower in a winter storm,
I wonder if the wind will ever be calm,
The bombs drop like rain,
Glory to Ukraine!

James A. Carter (USA)
Based in North Carolina, James is a retired English teacher. After thirty-five years of instructing English Composition and Literature, he has settled into a quiet life of books and cats and poetry.
E: jacarter1949@gmail.com

MOTHERS OF UKRAINE

When no-one is left to bury the dead, spectral voices shall rise
Free of flesh, unchained from eyes ashen in pale conformity.
And this chorus of the uncorporeal shall sing in splendor,
Swaddling the now silent earth in sound, thunder of longing,
Longing for the lost tongue, longing for love
That comes in notes of mourning, notes of madness
Keened in throats of mothers pressing ears to tender lips,
Listening, listening for sound, for breath,
But hearing only the ashen voice of death
Rendering the listener speechless.

Anne Maureen Medrano Esperidion (HONG KONG)
Originally from the Philippines, aspiring poet Anne has been in Hong Kong for seven years working as a domestic helper. Writing is her strength.
E: maureenanne090188@gmail.com

WHEN WILL PEACE REIGN

The sleeping volcano awaken
A placid terrain had been shaken
Howling blasts deafened the silence
Lightning flee in the sky's spacious fence

Roaring of the lion echoed through
Sirens sharp wailing never adieu
The hushed slumber haunted and troubled
Unrest fears and worries had doubled

Tears and longings keep rising on peaks
Bloody red brimming the sapphire creeks
Vast Greens ranges wilted and perished
downed are the skyscrapers we cherished

Chaos and turmoil stuffed the quite sphere
Noises of disputes all we can hear
Amity and unity faded
Singleness popped oneness invaded

When will we savour our peace again
When will these friendship and concord reign
Could care and love be our foods each day
So peace on earth find and gain its way

Anne Mitchell (USA)
Based in California, Anne's participation in a writing circle serve as both anchor and flame for curiosity to flourish and become poems.
E: annemitchell9@icloud.com
W: www.annemitchellpoetry.com

ALTERNATE UNIVERSE

Skim headlines then re-write the rosy side.
Your blue sky will come with the gold of spring.

Losses of winter disappear in spring-
babies are born, little hearts beat on.

Nation of lions, fierce hearts beat as one-
return to warm dens, victorious pride.

Melt snow into cups, hydrate in pride-
invaders fail, mass of spirit will thrive.

Children with crayons, thrive in sunflowers-
strike stick figure soldiers, colour not guns.

Fill trains with dead guns, tanks, send them back east.
Reunite families, let tables host feasts.

Ceasefire brings feast, replace missiles with grace.
The world will bring roses, honey of spring.

Adrienne Stevenson (CANADA)
Adrienne lives in Ontario. A retired forensic scientist, her poetry has appeared in more than 30 print and online publications. Her poem here is in memory of her Ukrainian grandmother.
E: adrienne@magma.ca
Twitter @ajs4t

UKRAINIAN NIGHTS 2022

they massed on our borders
we knew something bad was coming
but we found ways to ignore them
keep on living as if nothing
could actually happen

and when the bombs began
where were you? alone
or with others, maybe loved ones
whose death or injury
you feared more than your own

there was no warning of the first strike
though moments after it seemed
to have always been happening
minutes of anxiety between
instants of terror

I was sceptical of those
who spoke of trauma and stress
but now it is all too real
there is no going back
but we still face forward

we have been here before
suffered a madman's ire
starved in our millions
forced to become refugees
but we always return

and where were you then?
and where are you now?

I ask, but there are no answers

Fred Johnston (REPUBLIC OF IRELAND)

Born in Belfast, educated in Canada, now based in Ireland, Fred worked as a journalist for a number of years. He has published collections of poetry and short stories, as well as three novels.
E: greatfred7@gmail.com

WITNESS

My grand-uncle did not have the luxury
Of playing out his war on Facebook
Of weighing up this and conjecturing that
Or reloading Twitter to change the run of history

For him it was a a thing of three dimensions
The living madness of the shells, the horses cut
Screaming from the harness, a horse hanging
In a naked tree, this and more for lousy pensions

If only he could have sat and watched it on TV
Or just read the warrior songs the newspapers print
Ten thousand miles from where the dead lie and laugh
He might have lived a life of dull happiness and family

But the nightmares came in bright daylight
Half a century since they'd sent him home
As a teenager I stood witness to his trembling
The same age as he'd been when he went to fight

And when he died he was drunk and it was quick
He fell and that was that, an old man falling
So ordinary it made a joke of what he'd been
He left a stained pipe, a cap and a walking-stick

And here's a new war with new refugees and death
Not all that far from where he'd slept in mud
Place-names that even news-anchors can't pronounce
Old women and children walking nowhere, out of breath

Sophisticated commentary, bombs that think
Spin and lies and half-truths, angels, devils, God Himself
Image-makers, drone footage, death cleaned up
A video-game war for children, without the blood and stink

The enemy is over there, and we are over here
Just like a hundred years ago, not much has changed
What's really happening, no one knows -
Ask the elderly teenage warrior, sick with fear.

Daniel de Culla (SPAIN)
Daniel is a writer, poet, painter and photographer. He has participated in a number of international poetry and theatre festivals, and has collaborated with magazines and journals worldwide.
E: gallotricolor@yahoo.com

ALARM! WAR!

They are there the criminals of war
With their bombardments stunning
The sky and the cities of Ukraine.
Opposites what do they do?
Opposites are made
To the sound of weapons
And they are just as criminals of war
That they.
Their arrogance is useless
Nor their threats of sentences
Well they are dismayed
And they stay scared
Leaving the field free
To crime and vile murder
Of a defenceless population
Who sees his honour, his country and his life
Hanging from the barrels of tanks
As if those were cat fur.
As always some condemn
And others applaud and bless
That's how bad humans are!
While the echo of the bombs
They hear resound
In villages, in towns and cities
Seriously raise their necks
Those who take part
In these joys of war
And their weapons factories.
Who would believe that in the 21st century
Being smart
As they say we are humans
One another
Scale regions, countries and nations
With panic, terror, crime and fear!
So bad are those criminals
Eastern frights
Like the ones in the west
So scary

Only for the desire to steal, loot
And annihilate nations
To achieve an empire.
Damned they are!

Fahredin Shehu (KOSOVO)
Fahredin is an internationally renowned poet. He has authored over 20 books, and his poetry has been translated into 30 languages.
E: drita.islame@gmail.com
W: www.fekt.org

ONE DAY

See if I can compare
my days of horror with
the blast that brought
the pieces of brain
of an infant in
my empty hands
empty of all tools
absent for evildoing
the angst in a dream seen
nine months before the real
thing happened 22 years ago
I see on this day
thrice repeated deed of mischief
hard, very hard to experience
the same ache of War on my
Body of Humankind
when the wind blows in the East
the pain I feel on my right
when the wind blows in the West
the pain I feel on my left
when I see death of children
from Nadir to Horizon
a muttered voice from my
heart's void breaks the heavy
Gates of Heaven, all made of Lebanese Cedar
with the golden clutches dismantled to pieces
one day it'll happen ...
one day on the golden shore
one day it'll happen ...
one day, one day of a Men's year
shall rejoice life and living adore
for no greed is a salvation and
no bloodshed is a bliss
for there's no wound on earth
that did not ache on my Humankind Being

Eric Lawson (USA)
Based in California, Eric's work as appeared in a number of magazines, literary journals and poetry platforms worldwide.
E: lawson_eric@hotmail.com

LAST TRAIN TO UKRAINE

You might say what's the big deal
You've tuned out from what you feel
But those helpless folks in Ukraine
are dying under a Russian boot heel

Putin thinks he's clever and cute
With his ego and thousand-dollar suit
No more negotiations, it's all mute
He's a twenty-first century brute

We'll steer that train under water
and over the highest mountains
We're on a mission of love, friends
No stopping at Swiss fountains

We need to send in the Red Cross
and let the wounded people out
"As long as there are Ukrainians
there is a Ukraine," the people shout

You might be saying what's the use
Next it'll be Crimea or Belarus
But when the innocents are massacred
how the hell can you even refuse?

We need more flowers and candy
not a growing stockpile of more guns

Let's unleash our imaginations and
help those in need without the funds

We'll take the last train to Ukraine
We've got whiskey to dull the pain
We'll save our brothers and sisters
before democracy goes down the drain

All aboard for a mighty rescue trip
The convoy stretches a hundred miles long
Won't you help me to help Ukraine
Won't you all help me to sing this song

Sabyasachi Nazrul (BANGLADESH)
Based in Shariatpur, poet Sabyasachi has co-authored 17 books, and authored two of his own. His work has been published in national newspapers of Bangladesh, and in journals worldwide.
E: no17nazrul@gmail.com

STOP FIGHTING, STOP FIGHTING

The collapse of the Soviet Union,
and so did Stalin;
You are on the way to destruction.
Why do you want to occupy land of Ukraine?
Child body is burning,
Humanity is burning,
All are destroying;
Why even say Stop the War,
You don't hear that's!
An abominable bandit monster
You are a man-eater,
In the eyes of male female and children
The water is dripping.
I say Putin Ukraine is your ancestors?
Stop fighting stop fighting ;
I don't want war anymore.
I want peace, peace and peace.

Sally Zakariya (USA)
Based in Virginia, Sally 's poetry has appeared in over 90 print and online journals.
E: sally.zakariya@gmail.com
W: www.butdoesitrhyme.com

LEAVING UKRAINE 2022

The turn of winter, the cusp of spring
snow trampled, smudged, bloodied

Around you a dirge of shrieking sirens
percussion of artillery shells

Beneath you the beat of train on tracks
as you flee from a broken city …
flee seeking shelter in another land
with a cousin you barely remember

Now a curtain of dust and smoke
clouds what is left … the rubble …
the deaths … the duty to resist

Everything once was blue as morning

Gary Shulman, MS. Ed (USA)
Based in New York, Gary was a Social Services and Training Director for Resources for Children with Special Needs, and has spent a lifetime supporting vulnerable families and children.
E: shulman.gary@yahoo.com

MY HEART BLEEDS

Humankind-a massive mistake
For lessons of history seem never learned
Diversity scorned children still burned
What is the answer to murderous choices
How do you cope when death still rejoices
At sights of suffering mother and child
Victims of those whose souls are now blind
To compassion, to reason, to kindness to love
Is there a miracle from spirits above?
History repeats, lessons never seemed learned
Diversity scorned and children still burned
Will humanity ever turn this around?
It seems no peace shall ever be found!
I have no answers, just one simple plea
Keep your hatred within ... just let others be!
As history has taught us, that's merely a dream
For humanity learns little
Evil minds will still scheme
I don't know the answer
I just feel the pain
My heart just bleeds
For the people of Ukraine

Bhuwan Thapaliya (NEPAL)
Bhuwan is a poet from Kathmandu, and works as an economist. He is the author of four poetry collections, and his work has been published worldwide.
E: nepalipoet@yahoo.com

THE SUNFLOWERS WILL DANCE AGAIN

The war will end someday
and they'll sing and dance again.
But you may not be there
to hold my hand
and I may not be there
to sing our song that day.

The war will end someday
though we may not be there
to witness the end of the war
and pose for the selfies
and smile at the birds,
flying low over their head
carrying sunflower seeds
in their beaks.

The war will end someday
and as bleached statues
brutally stained by the
voracious tongue
of the harsh winter
we may stare
at the world
with long cycles
of drought in our eyes.

The war will end someday
but we may live
in the coil of confinement
and may not flap our wings
for many, many years.

The war will end someday.
Ugly, serrated, blood-curdling tongue
of the Russian tanks lurking in Ukraine
to ruthlessly serve Putin's insatiability
can never silence the Sunflower's song.
The sunflowers will dance again.

They will embrace our dreams
and invigorate our hope evermore.

The Sunflowers are
an eternity in themselves.

Jason Kirk Bartley (USA)
Based in Ohio, Jason is an Christian poet with a Master's degree in leadership and ministry.
E: jaskirk@live.com

UKRAINIAN BROTHERS & SISTERS

As your flag of yellow and blue,
flutters in the air,
We stand with Ukraine and our
brothers and sisters over there.
Ukrainian brothers and sisters,
do not hang your heads in pain.
Nothing goes unnoticed,
nothing goes in vain.
God smiles down on you.
Soon it'll all be through,
your bravery ever tested,
on your shoulders,
your country's
future has rested,
praying for your peace,
that the wars and battles cease.
We love you each and everyone.
Take care, but thank someone.
With freedom the pricetag is life,
sorry about all your strife.
As bombs burst in the air,
your freedom you declare.
We say a little prayer,
for God gives his biggest battles
to his few that are faithful.
Sometimes life is so cruel.
Hang in there and love one another.
You'll always be our sisters and our
brothers.

Krishna Kumar Srinivasan (INDIA)
Krishna lives in Pune. He has been writing poems since he was 10 years-old, and has compiled a collection of poems spanning 50 decades. His work has been published in various international media.
E: krsnarti@gmail.com

THE TREE AND AN OLD WOMAN IN KIEV

Yesterday it was raining leaves;
Mostly dried ones.
Yellowing or yellowed
some green too.
a few new happy leaves.
Leaves that have lived
their life stuck to a branch.

Her 81 year old eyes
Had seen innumerable seasons
Of growing, falling, growing leaves
On the tree that stretched its arms
To hold her hand as it grew old with her

She loved to sit on her couch
looking out the large glass window
at birds blindly pecking and flapping
their wings against the glass.
And then cuddling themselves
On the tree.

Today the bombing of the city
unexpectedly by friends
across from the other side
surprised her.
The entire side of the building
collapsed.
Glass shattering like
melting chocolate lava cake.
She was irritated by the dust
that accumulated on her couch
as she sipped on her cold coffee.
The electricity was impossible to fix
because the cables had burnt.
Once in a while surprised birds
would fly in, amused at
their flight of freedom.
Bird poops adorned the shelves where

the candle wax had melted

The birds and the old woman
were resettling inside
their new abode -
A hole on the floor that was once her
apartment.

The tree though stood there
Burnt, black, charred.
It will never rain leaves ever again.

Brajesh Singh (INDIA)
Based in Lucknow, Brajesh is a writer, poet and translator. He has won a number of international awards, and his poems have appeared in anthologies, magazines and journals worldwide.
E: nepalipoet@yahoo.com
FB: @Brajesh Singh

A MESSENGER KID

O! Man
If you are literate enough
read the message on a poster
in the hands of a messenger kid
standing on the gate of his broken home,
a baby in the lap of his mother
and her eyes are full of tears.

Stop the war
No more war
War is a crime against humanity
Destroys peace, harmony, and prosperity.

With rising sun from the east,
as if returning of little Buddha,
encourages world for peace and harmony
and fades away the dark cloud of *Yuddha*.

Bruce W. Niedt (USA)
Bruce lives in New Jersey and is a retired Federal employee. His poetry has appeared in dozens of magazines and journals, and his first full-length collection has just been released.
E: jackbugs@comcast.net
W: www.bniedt.blogspot.com
FB: @bruceniedt1

A WHITE PIANO IN KHARKIV

The boy plays deliberately,
a plaintive tune by Philip Glass,
the phrases repeating like echoes
from a white grand piano
in a hotel lobby,

while not far away, rockets rip apart
the facades of apartment blocks.

He continues to play,
fingers in a slow dance across the keys,
on an instrument like an island of snow
in the middle of a filigreed sea of carpet,
for one last moment of peace.

Gordon J Simmonds (ENGLAND)
Gordon lives in Lincolnshire. His first poem was recited on BBC Schools radio way back in 1963. He has had a large number of poems published since, and in 2016 he published his first anthology.
E: gj.simmonds@outlook.com
FB: @gj.simmonds

MORE OLD SOLDIERS THOUGHTS

So much I've writ and thought and said,
'Gainst war, futility and much untimely death,
Yet even as these words I write, the Warlords rise once more.
By power and evil hatred driven mad
These dogs of war betray their warrior heroes past.
Across Ukrainian plains they stride
For each atrocious act from which they draw their pride
As would some morbid craftsman to a willing master,
Declare a job well done.
Whence all those willing helpers come, I do not know.
So many deaf to children's cries and mother's pleas
And blind to ragged ruins of wretched suffering and pain.
I wish it were my power to say, 'Be done.
No beast to these dark depths would bring his fellow beasts,
So let not power by man reduce his fellow man.'
And when these soft spoke words are done,
The stick from its dark scabbard drawn, must rise
To strike the evil from the hearts of those who will not hear.
And in the great arena show,
The warlords and their mighty cohorts where
God's great dream of right and wrong doth draw the line.
I hear the cries of men who would have peace,
Who think 'Desist. Desist' when shouted loud and long
Will save us from the dark ambitions of wicked men,
E'en when the dagger to the heart is plunged to the hilt
They cry 'Desist'.
Our wish for peace, for love and harmony to reign
Is deep within each human heart entrained,
So how are we, in innocence and dread, to know
Just when, to the tormentor talk, or make relentless war.
As this old soldier ponders twixt the two, the test
Within this faulted fathers conscience says:
'Now that I'm too old to fight,
My son, go out and help to put things right.'

Bozena Helena Mazur-Nowak (ENGLAND/POLAND)
Originally from Opole in Poland, Bozena has published seven volumes of poetry. She has also published a novel, and a number of short story collections.
E: bozena.mazur-nowak@hotmail.co.uk
FB: @bozenahelenam

HOW CAN I TELL YOU, SON?

How can I tell you, my son,
that there is no home anymore,
that your rocking horse got burned,
that I haven't anything to eat for you?
How can I tell you, son,
that the roof from which we used to watch
the starry sky completely collapsed a day before?
How can I tell you, son,
that you can't see your beloved grandma anymore?
She was trapped and died under the rubble of the house.
How can I tell you, son,
that grandfather has gone forever too?
He went to save grandma but instead
died burned alive.
How can I tell you, son,
that there is no street on which you grew up,
and you knew so well each corner of it?
How can I tell you, son,
that daddy went to Heaven last night?
He died in the hospital saving other people's lives,
while it was bombed by an enemy.
How can I tell you, my son,
that you have to live on,
although the world is dying around now,
though the world is burning?
Though you are a kid now, remember,
the immortal spirit still lives in us.
It connects us in need and allows us to survive
no matter how tough our life is now.
We will defeat the Monster,
which has attacked insidiously during the night,
and we will be living in the land of our
ancestors, as it is our land and belongs to us!

Michael Claxton (JAPAN)
Born in London, Michael grew up in Europe as a professional musician and has lived in Japan for about twenty years. He has published 14 books of poetry.
E: michael.claxton@i.softbank.jp
Amazon: @B094J5DRWK
W: www.theeyeshaveitalwaysfavourites.tumblr.com
W: www.theeyeshaveitalwaysplaces.tumblr.com
W: www.theeyeshaveitalwaystoo.tumblr.com
W: www.thereisjoyinrepetition.tumblr.com

UKRAINE IS RUSSIA

Ukraine is Russia
Ukrainians are Russians.
And if they don't believe me,
if they don't accept this
then I will send young Russians,
young conscripts, on a training mission
to kill them.
Apartment buildings, shopping centres,
schools and kindergartens,
maternity hospitals.
All fair game.
Bombard them into believing.
(Vladimir)
Ukraine is a very large country
Ukraine has a proud history
Ukraine's proud people are
being murdered,
murdered to
satisfy the
ego of a short, megalomaniac who pretends that USSR
history is his raison d'être when in fact it is his
failure in, and the lack of respect he felt was
owed him in, the KGB in St. Petersburg.
Vladimir, how do you sleep at night?
Do you really sleep well at night?
Unfortunately, highly likely.

Chester Civelli (SWITZERLAND)
Chester is a poet and singer-songwriter based in Sierre. He has released two poetry books, and has had poems featured in various webzines and magazines.
E: chester.civelli@gmail.com
FB : @PoetryReadingOnline
Instagram: @poetry_reading_online

BORDERLANDS

I.

This is your name
But a border
For whom
Between what
Between *us*
And *them*

Then who are you
For *us*
For *them*

The middle empire
Of modern warfare

This will hold 'em back
We said

This
Is what holds us back
Now

Pushed the pencil
In our closed eyes
Blaming someone else
For our bleeding

II.

Watch them come
From all around the world
Your *brothers*
Your *sisters*
... of colour...

This colour that brings us closer to the heart while others are stranger

Heroes of one nation
Under the stars
Shining bright at night
On your TV screen
Reminding you
Whom you should cry for

This is threatening the world
They say
Our world
I say

All wars threaten *the* world

Javisth Bhugobaun (MAURITIUS)
Javisth is an 18 year-old poet and a student of literature. He lives in Quatre-Bornes. His dream has always been to be a poet and let the world hear his words, and hope that his words will help others.
E: javisth03@gmail.com

SURVIVAL

Like birds of the same feather
We flee together
Under the black sun.
Avoiding where pots and pans clang.
Jumping over fences.
Hiding in the house of the neighbour
That we hated, hoping that a nightingale
Does not sing.
As silent as lambs,
We shush our breath,
So that the rustling of dead leaves,
Hide our fate and let us live another nightmare,
But
The crushing of the cracked glass
Under our feet swollen
Makes our shadow light in the dark.
And like moles, we dig ourselves
A way to a bright day
And let our lineage seep
between the needles of our teeth.

Chad Norman (CANADA)
Based in Nova Scotia, Chad has had three poetry collections published, and has just completed his fourth. He has given talks and reading across Canada and Europe.
E: namronskichacha@gmail.com
FB: @chad.norman.96780

NO OTHER DESCRIPTION THAN DISBELIEF
For a President

As flakes of snow remain falling
the cardinal returns to turn blue
feeding fearlessly at the yellow feeder.
Imagination allows this for one man
full of feeling more than helpless
at a window where he also sees a war.

His hands are empty but something is felt there
perhaps as the blue beak is sorting seeds
a moment will arrive when hope will adjust
the colour of those wings, all the feathers
handling the weight of winter's invasion.

Rebecca Lowe (WALES)
Rebecca is a freelance editor, poet, spoken word event organiser and publisher. She has been widely published, both nationally and internationally, and her poetry has been featured BBC's radio 3 and 4.
E: swanmedia@ntlworld.com
FB: @rebecca.lowe.poetry
Instagram: @BeckyLowePoet
Twitter @BeckyLowePoet
YouTube: @Becky Lowe Swansea

THE SEEDS OF PEACE

On the week when bombs rained down
their bitter litany of anger and fear,
A choir opened its lungs in a city square
and sang of freedom

On the night when families fled
to basements and bunkers
beneath the exploding streets,
A mother cried her birth pangs,
And a baby trembled into the warmth
of her waiting arms

On the day when soldiers
lined the streets with Kalashnikovs,
A grandmother planted sunflower seeds
and prayed she would live to see them bloom

And it is always this way,
This blossoming of hope in the darkest times,
When love itself feels an act of rebellion,
We will always be here:
Singing our songs of freedom,
Planting the seeds of Peace.

William Khalipwina Mpina (MALAWI)
William is a poet, fiction writer, Economist and Data Analyst. Many of his works appear in international literary magazines, and has contributed verses in a number of anthologies.
E: williammpina3@gmail.com
FB: @Khalipwina.Mpina
Twitter: @William.Mpina

WAR

My husband waves
Us to go ...
Go, go, go ...
My husband says
War is coming
Like butterflies
Russian helicopters
Are flying fast
My husband urges
Us to flee ...
While he, himself
Does not want
To leave ...
He runs towards
A flying bullet
And he cries -
My Ukraine!
My people!
My Ukraine!
My land!
Hugging it
He drops dead
In a pool
Of his own blood
My husband died
For peace to return
In Ukraine.

We shall dance in blood

The rivers are dry
Well, we are not worried
We have our blood to try

The cities are empty
Yes because we have shellers

They have upon them a duty

To turn us into wailers
We shall dance in blood
Till they are satisfied

Karen Douglass (USA)
Karen is based in Colorado. She has been a psychiatric nurse, horsewoman, racetrack judge, mother (still is), college instructor, poet, and novelist.
E: kvdbooks@gmail.com

ART BRINGS NO PEACE

Symphony no distraction,
though song draws no blood
and breaks no bones,
we cannot warble our way
out of war.
      The poet's pen
breaks no bones, but
deflects not one bullet,
words a little box of bandages
to staunch bloody fear,
return the routines of peace,
the news full of sports scores
instead of body counts.

Alicja Maria Kuberska (POLAND)
Based in Warsaw, Alicja is an award-winning poet, novelist, journalist and editor, and has had her poetry published in a number of international anthologies and magazines.
E: alicja107@vp.pl
FB: @alicja.kuberska.7

I'M CRYING FOR YOU, UKRAINE

My life is like a broken window pane
- dreams crumbled into rain from crumbs
and memories hurt painfully.

The view outside the window
is the same and not the same.
Trunks of burned trees
stick up like exclamation marks,
the blind eyes of the houses
stare blankly ahead.

I can't hear the birds
and the chirping of the children.
The silence is interrupted
by the wail of the alarm sirens
and the terrifying
whistle of falling bombs.

How to pack the past into one suitcase?
How do I tell my child,
that there is no home left?
How to shut a torn door behind me?

Christopher Bogart (USA)
Christopher lives in New Jersey, and presently working on a Master of Fine Arts in Creative Writing. He has had work published internationally, and is working on his first novel.
E: cabogart@aol.com
FB: @Christopher-Bogart-Poet-Writer

SUNFLOWERS (Соняшники)

Across fields of Ukrayina,
Bright yellow heads atop green stalks,
Look up, defiant, at the sun.
They do not flinch, nor shy, nor run
From wind and rain.
They do not bend,
They do not break –
But face all that they're forced to face.
They stare into the solar fire,
Prepared for dangers from its glare.

They are *Ukrayins'ki sonyashnyky,*

The Golden Glory of All Ukraine.
Defend,
They must,
Their sacred Borderland.

Suzan Denis (CANADA)
Based in British Columbia , Suzan is compiling a collection of poems on recovery, and preparing to write a journey novel for a soul who reawakens the Garden of Eden within.
E: blessingsfromsuzan@gmail.com

CROSS THE LINE INTO A NEW BELONGING

Open the territory between us
Let the songs of our kin
Mingle in the fragrance of shared purpose

Could we join hands and hearts
Willing now to cross the line
Into a belonging that includes
Our collective stories of sorrow and loss
The search for meaning in the dark

Could we let go of the need to be right or wrong
As we sing and merge the fences between us

A new story unfolding

Ayesha Khurram (PAKISTAN)
Ayesha is a 16 year-old student and has been writing poems as a hobby since the age of nine. She is ambitious and passionate about her poetry, and has won many prizes in school for her work.
E: ashiak7786@gmail.com

DEATH!

The blazing sun burned his wounds,
His flesh had been torn by hounds,
The sound of shells and tanks made him cry,
He couldn't walk, he just couldn't even try,
His body deteriorated every minute,
His hope shattered every second,
Martyrs lay beside him covered in blood,
Thousands of families lost the ones they loved,
He wanted to escape this bitter reality,
He was a half dead boy no one would pity,
The atmosphere was covered with the scent of death,
It was a sight unbelievable, something like a myth,
And then there was a huge blast,
The little boy's soul departed at last!

Beata B. Agustin (PHILIPPINES)
Beata is a volunteer full-time church staff member, a teacher, a registered social worker, a writer, and is the resident poet of the Christian Bible Baptist Church in Laguna.
E: beatalovinghandscbbc@gmail.com

WE STAND FOR UKRAINE

We stand by faith in God for Ukraine's quest
Toward restoration of liberty
While overcoming conflict's painful test
As a nation of great sovereignty.

Toward restoration of liberty
Midst peaceful brotherly love's creed and deed
As a nation of great sovereignty
We pray for blessed unity indeed.

Midst peaceful brotherly love's creed and deed
Blended with virtue-exercise to reign
We pray for blessed unity indeed
Smiting selfishness and haughtiness-gain.

Blended with virtue-exercise to reign
Freedom-zeal wins over suppression blight
Smiting selfishness and haughtiness-gain
Since citizens want to enjoy truth's light.

Freedom-zeal wins over suppression blight
To let the world be inspired with peace-glow
Since citizens want to enjoy truth's light
Prevailing over hate-aggression blow.

To let the world be inspired with peace-glow
Around fervent global congenial ties
Prevailing over hate-aggression blow
Hope seeks legal sanctions to quell children's cries.

Around fervent global congenial ties
While overcoming painful conflict's test
Hope seeks legal sanctions to quell children's cries ...
We stand by faith in God for Ukraine's quest.

Barry Pittard (AUSTRALIA)
Barry is a retired teacher living in Queensland. He was also an actor, director and writer, and worked for a number of years as an NGO among forest tribes in India.
E: bpittard999@gmail.com

YOU ARE UKRAINE!

I'll jot late thoughts,
For I'll soon enough be gone ...
But you'll be here,
And you'll be soldiering on

If we sleep,
Imposters will steal our sleep.
If we creep,
Tyrant tigers leap

Ukraine!
You are throat for the voiceless
When some voices dare not speak,
Ukraine!
You are hope of whole countries
Against bullies with a madness streak

You are Ukraine!
You are Nightingale
That can turn into Eagle,
You are Ukraine
In the flash of a moment
When once you are beleaguered

If we oversleep,
We are slaughtered easy as sheep.
If we creep,
Tyrant tigers leap.

But you'll be here,
And you'll be soldiering on.

Stephen Kingsnorth (WALES / ENGLAND)
Born in London, Stephen retired with Parkinson's Disease to Wales from ministry in the Methodist Church. He has had over 300 pieces published in journals, anthologies and on poetry websites.
E: slkingsnorth@googlemail.com
W: www.poetrykingsnorth.wordpress.com

A BRIDGE TO FAR

For fear of tank tracks lurching on,
invading caterpillars' roll -
but butterflies never on wing -
one blew the bridge, he bombed himself,
to halt the onslaught, 'special op'.

So now there's reach, route through the swell,
those refugees who walk the plank,
awash with anger, fear, despair,
the only spin, tyred wheelchair bound,
as drawn both lame, halt, over whirl.

Though self-inflicted wound of war,
cut artery that might survive,
this is a channel, stepping stones,
trudged ballet balance, above the roar,
footpath one wide, in measured creep.

The sirens call above the waves
and soon submerged, protect from fire,
but streaming queues, their bridge to far,
though poles apart find open arms,
embrace in place of armaments.

So straddle up, and mount the blocks,
cross river, course towards the sea,
delivered by a forded place,
the cost, encounter, fly by nights,
a last stand before curtain fall.

Will hedgehogs lie, flat squashed on road -
tank traps, trench warfare, urban scape,
Odesa file, sand, blizzard bagged,
fight on the beaches, echo, thrall,
yet cyberwarfare in the air.

This text is delayed telegram,

a war despatch, front, living room,
as blitzkrieg bogged, guerrilla war;
campaign of days can creep to years,
or you may read brief history.

Deborah Hefferon (USA)
Deborah is a recently retired cross-cultural communication trainer based in Washington, DC. She has worked in the field of international education in over 70 countries, including Ukraine.
E: DeborahHefferon@gmail.com

SUNDAY MORNING

Since the pandemic, rituals have become more ingrained.
And somehow sweeter, like a rich plum cake soaked in rum, rediscovered at the back of the fridge - better than I remember. I sneak out of the sheets and slip into yesterday's outfit, wheel the squeaky cart to the supermarket that connects with my apartment building underground. The store is empty like I sought in the feverish days of Covid. Now I care less, trust in the science, still wear my mask. The shelves are stocked this week (looking 30 minutes ahead; I will have crossed everything off my list). How can I not think about the Ukrainian refugees flinging themselves across Europe? Which country do you prefer to go to? What colour bell peppers do you want, madam? Paper or plastic?

My husband makes blueberry pancakes and decorates the plates with other fruits: pineapple triangles, blackberries, apple chunks. He uses real butter and store brand syrup; I use soy butter and expensive maple syrup. I've lost the origin story of our preferences. I imagine how grateful the refugees will be in Poland or Romania for the offer of a cup of hot tea. Their choices are growing slimmer by the hour, the babies scream as one. After glancing at the newspaper, shielding my eyes from the larger-than-normal headlines and graphic photos to bring the war into our living rooms, we walk to the National Cathedral. We don't enter the church, but instead sit in the Bishop's Garden to admire signs of spring: butter yellow paper bushes, brave daffodils and grounded bluets. I find myself in prayer, connected to those on their way.

Charo Gabay Sidon (SINGAPORE/ PHILIPPINES)
Born in the Philippines, currently working as a domestic worker in Singapore, Charo enjoys writing, and has contributed to a number of poetry publications.
E: sidoncharo9@gmail.com
FB: @aileen.gabay.7

HOLD ON UKRAINE

Hold strong Ukraine!
The love, courage, respect and determination of your people will lead you in more peaceful future.
Stay strong!
Fight with a good fight!

You are brave!
Your countrymen are ready to sacrifice themseves for their loved ones, and this country.
To get the freedom and democracy to have peace.
And to come out of this conflict relatively whole.

Stand still beloved country of Ukraine!
Your people love and need you!
Your hero soldiers will depend you.
Big respect and honour to all soldiers and civilians who fought your good fight!
To get what this country needs.

Hold on Ukraine!
Prayers and sympathy to all your brave people
Keep fighting and believing that your battle will soon end up successful.
May God bring peace to your country Ukraine, and to the entire world.

Estelle Phillips (ENGLAND)
Multi-award winning writer and poet Estelle has had her work published in a large number of journals and magazines worldwide, as well as on the BBC. She is finalizing her debut novel.
E: estelleathalterworth@yahoo.co.uk
Instagram @estelle_writer4
Twitter @legalimportant

REAPER

"My name is Ihr, I'm sergeant of National Guard. My nickname is Reaper."
He spoke quickly but slowed to enunciate his name
and pride hinted from his syllables "Reeperr".
Bravery in his voice harrowed the soil he stood upon,
soil stained with blood and knitted with bones from the Holodomor,
flexing now against the grind of tanks instructed by a cornered rat.
Reaper's courage sounded through the radio into my kitchen,
climbed the back of my neck and goose pimpled the hairs on my arms.
I shivered with his proclamation, *"we fight like lions"*

and Reaper is my son walking to school on his first day,
his small hand clutched mine
but when we said good-bye he did not look back.
Reaper is other mothers' sons walking to war

and he is my father
watching the world with sorrow, the television on full volume
to obliterate the sound of his father in the water after his ship was torpedoed,
and all other fathers straightening their backs to stand and fight
in the forests and fields, on the shores and streets.

Reaper is my lover
facing the bear with only his hands and ready to die protecting his land.
He is others' lovers' sacrifice

and Reaper is brother to Taras Shevchenko, *"wedded to a life that's free".*

NOTE: Reaper is about a Ukrainian soldier who was interviewed by the BBC. It references the "Holodomor" which was the "famine genocide" of Ukrainians caused by Stalin. Putin is described as a "cornered rat" because of Putin's brag that he learnt a lesson from a rat he trapped: the rat had nowhere to go so it turned and attacked Putin. President Volodymyr Zelenskyy's speech to the House of Commons is referenced and "Taras Shevchenko" is Ukraine's famous poet who championed independence.

Previous publication: *Reaper* was first published by BBC Radio Wiltshire who broadcast the work on 17th March 2022, and a poetry film was subsequently released to YouTube.

Gloria Sofia (NETHERLANDS / CAPE VERDE)
Originally from Cape Verde, Glória has had her work published in various international magazines and websites, and has participated in a number of international poetry festivals.
E: gloriasvmonteiro@gmail.com
W: www.gloriasvmonteiro.wixsite.com/gloriasofia
FB: @autoragloriasofia

OH DEATH!

Oh Death!
When this day comes
I will rise haughtily
I will walk with courage
graceful as the running clouds
in the sky
I will receive you as the beloved land of
pleasure
just to welcome the sun
Death, oh Death!
I will seduce you
opening the button on my chest
stripping myself of fear and anguish
in the whisper of the eyes
I will give you time to savour
you will sink the end into me
moaning from the cold and consuming heat
I will cling to you with fragile arms
and I will cry out the sweet melody:
"Take away the father, take away mother and children"
if your coldness did not lie
in the rivers of my veins
I would rise and beat you
with my kisses
I'd kill you with my love
Oh unjust death!

Lily Swarn (INDIA)
Lily is an internationally acclaimed multilingual poet, author, columnist and radio show host. She has published five books, and has won over 50 international awards.
E: sukhish83@gmail.com

UKRAINE

Where will you hide me in this tormented city?
Raining death, collecting shrapnel
Bruising humanity with power games

I've seen your lugubrious countenance
Sedated with Shanti mantras and chants on YouTube

I've heard your baby's anguished cries
As you try and flee from your wounded homeland

Melting snow to drink
Chopping wood to cook

Don't forget to pack your childhood in your knapsack
You can't leave it gasping for breath amidst horrendous bombs

Walk away with your mama's fervent prayers,
Your father's jocund guffaws ringing in your ears

Stride into the warmth of the reassuring sun
Keep your feet warmly shod in the icy weather of cruelty

Xavier Panadès I Blas (WALES / SPAIN)

Catalan born, now based in Wales, Xavier has been instrumental in the internationalisation the culture of Catalan. He is internationally published, and is regularly booked at poetry festivals and events.
E: xpan100@gmail.com
W: www.xpan.bandcamp.com
FB: @SuperPanades
Instagram: @super_xavier

WAITING, WAITING, WAITING ...

This morning is different,
anguish has frozen hearts,
the earth has absolved sorrow,
beauty shines in the dark.

In Kiev the scourge of bombs
slaughter the soul of the streets.
In Mariúpol the persistent bullets
empty the buildings of humanity.

Love has been hidden underground
between the roots of the trees,
from the transvestite truth,
from the horror of bloody words.

The loss of earthly desires
has been replaced by longing.
Longing for love, longing for peace,
longing for silence, longing for light.

Time is just a wind
vindicating the inheritance of the heart.
The moment has become the place
where reality and hope are antonyms.

Walls suppurate the innocent blood
of the enemies of war.
The ruins hide the bodies
of the allies of peace and brotherhood.

The words of fraternity from the West,
are the sound of an imaginary rain,
are chants without music or passion,
are the echoes of forced loneliness.

Like drops escaping from a tap,
lives become ghosts,
illusions rot in vain,
innocence is exiled from cruelty.

And what has become of the Ukrainians?
They lick the horror of the wounds,
cry out in anger against the enemy;
and waiting for the chess game to end,
to bury the coffins of the dead ...

Vanessa Caraveo (USA)
Based in Texas, Vanessa is an award-winning author and published poet. She is involved with various organizations that assist children and adults with disabilities.

IN THE STREETS OF UKRAINE

The innocents in the streets of Ukraine
scream out in defiance and pain,
their peace stolen, shattered, discarded.

All because one man was paranoid
and didn't give his nation a choice.
A war that no one even believes in
paints homes red like a crimson wind.
Sinless lives all suddenly end.

Gone, gone, those days of peace.
Memories in the rearview now.
Blood fills what were happy streets
and all the world is asking how
Ukraine could possibly survive.

Do they not deserve to thrive?
They only want to stay alive.
Alone they fight, stumble, and strive.

But good will soon prevail
and gone will be the days
innocent lives are bravely sacrificed
to bring what is desperately needed.
Peace and unity for all in this world.

Irma Kurti (ITALY / ALBANIA)
Based in Bergamo, Irma is a poet, writer, lyricist, journalist, and translator. She has published 24 books in Albanian, 17 in Italian and 6 in English, and has written about 150 lyrics for adults and children.
E: kurtial@yahoo.com
FB: @IrmaKurtiAutore
Instagram: @irma.kurti

IN A MEADOW OF DREAMS

I heard near and distant gunshots,
that tonight chased away the peace.
In the fake silence surrounding me
was heard only my heartbeat.

The cry of a child followed them
just like a sad and broken melody.
Immersed in the dark of thoughts
I hid the pain and anguish in a tear.

Do not break that child's sleep,
life is a charming fairy tale for him,
let him wander in a dream's meadow,
where only green and quietness drip.

Soon the dawn will wipe off my tears
and I'll begin to dream as that child.
My hopes are like confused clouds
after the storm in a dark gloomy sky.

Tonight, someone killed my sleep,
my fatigued eyes fix on the horizon:
The sky is an immense bloody shirt,
little by little there the sun is rising.

Hillol Ray (USA)
Based in Texas, Hillol is a poet laureate, author, song writer, and multi-linguist. He received letters of personal compliments for his poems from former U.S. President Bill Clinton, former U.S. Vice President and Nobel Peace Laureate Al Gore.
W: www.bwesner.wixsite.com/hillolrayawards
W: www. bwesner.wixsite.com/hillolraypoetry

WAR AND WELTANSCHAUUNG

Since the prehistoric dawn, war seems to be
An integral part of global mankind-
And evidences are too many, as on history pages
We can always read or find!
The cause of wars may brew on simple issues,
With the exception of a trifling few-
While the showdown of powers agitate the nations
In no time for a global view!

'Name-calling' may be the underlying fibers
To weave the threads of secret war-
And diplomacies begin to clip the 'weeds'
Like the mulching blade in a lawnmower!
Man can put many names to prospective enemies
And the 'trick' grows like a malaise-
While the signals for their destructions
Are carried out without any mercy or a praise!

Our primitive brains can still do to others
What the tribesmen did for recreation or food-
By beheading a fellow man and eat his brain out
For a display of super power or mood!
For modern warfare, soldiers are prepared
By constantly cleaning their rifles and boot-
Followed by incessant running through obstacle course
And making them expert to shoot!

The practice goes on by drilling thousand times
Until the wary brain is reduced to orders-
And become imperative to kill the enemies
By any means, within or outside the borders!
"Hillolscope" reveals that we have not changed much
Since our obscure prehistoric days-
And we call it now "Weltanschauung"
To glorify the imperialism like the bright sunrays!

Those who resent injustice and mistreatment
Are labelled as the enemy for the battle-
While those who are the followers or puppets
Of the mighty flock like a herd of cattle!
We see in a monopoly of power today,
Those with richness and bigger arms or firepower-
Have flocked together against majority
Who resent global empire run from ivory tower!

Armies are engaged to kill or maim the enemies
Before they return with glorious smiles-
But eternity will remain and millions of flowers
Will bloom in the oasis of skeleton piles!
The dead will remain dead and the victors will return
To chew their shame till the old age-
While humans will speak again and again,
And commit same nonsense for a history page!

At the footsteps of fundamentalism, the latent war
Between the believers and the infidels-
Seem to mesmerize the world today
While the weapons of mass destruction ring the bells!
As per our anthropological knowledge,
We all belong to the same genome since our birth-
Irrespective of belief, God has not chosen any people
Or religion to be imposed on Earth!

Neuroscience thinks drug addict can kick habit
To replace addiction for mysticism or fun-
'Cause the brain damaged in biochemical metabolism
Needs a source of 'high' on the run!
Mystical ecstasies, acceptable for the believers,
Are in contradiction with "normal" brain-
Followed by truths and common beliefs of mankind,
Like water swirling down the drain!

Under "Hillolscope", the "fundamentalist" ideas
Are the real danger to global mankind-
While the "religious madness" protrudes its ugly head
In world politics to put us in bind!
A justification of genocide based on the race,
Religion or colour should never be a "must"-
To feed or meet the ego of imperial needs,
Aimed at secret aggressions or monetary lust!

Present madness to alluding to war might make us

To believe only the strong can be good-
But that will never last forever, 'cause heaven will plunge,
And it's the thought for food!
Those who are now trying to grab the whole world
In both hands should think it well,
That those who tried that in the past are vaguely respected,
Or our mind does not dwell!

Remember, for only those that advocate the good
Seem to remain in the memory lane-
Irrespective of variable turbulence
From war and Weltanschauung, like a lion's mane!

Eithne Cullen (ENGLAND / REPUBLIC OF IRELAND)
Originally from Ireland, now based in London, Eithne has written two novels and a book of short stories, and has published internationally. She also contributes as an editor to a writing magazine.
E: eithnemac@ntlworld.com
Instagram: @eithnecullen57
Twitter: @eithne_cullen

PEACE INSTEAD

Names of the fallen etched in stone
dying in foreign fields, alone
give comfort for those left at home

but turn our thoughts to peace instead
where lives aren't ruined by bloodshed
harmony and tranquillity are spread

poppies, red as blood are laid
blessings muttered, prayers prayed
memories must never fade

Beverly M. Collins (USA)
Beverly is an award-winning poet and the author of two books. Based in California, her work has appeared in magazines and journals worldwide.
E: clearandtrue@aol.com
W: www.beverlym-collins.pixels.com
FB: @beverlymcollinsnow

ENDANGERED

Oh, the spin of tiny razor-beliefs that deeply
Cut

Away the happiness that could've
Made many long sweet memories …
Stood

Like the steel monkey, trapped in the path of
compressor wheels that screamed in the key of
Red

Then, searched like a lighthouse without a lamp … Knew
darkness just as a wingless bird in a tiger pit learns
Terror

Endangered; like a secret whispered (whose quiet
exploded and became the centre-of-attention) gets…
Unchained

This is you, me, us, mine, yours and ours.

Francisc Edmund Balogh (ROMANIA)
Based in Satu Mare, Francisc is an award-winning poet, writer and musician, and has been published in various international anthologies and literary magazines.
E: franciscbalogh42@gmail.com
FB: @francisc.e.balogh

DISARMED

The guns fell soft onto the ground,
upon the mother's heart, turning into flowers,
the soldiers rose like clouds above us
and cried the blue out of the sky,
love remained a sad bird, encaged,
life was hanging on the string of the break of dawn,
the light was crawling ragged, riddled
ready to give it's last breath,
happiness's destiny got stuck in
it's own unbeaten path.

Low Kian Seh (SINGAPORE)

Low Kian Seh is poet, writer and a chemistry teacher by occupation. He won first prize in Singapore's National Poetry Competition. His works had been published in a number of anthologies and magazines.
E: kianseh@gmail.com
W: www.kianseh.me

WELL-WISHES FOR A WEDDING

the groom brought forward his wedding
date because a brighter tomorrow

may not come, months later. together,
groom and bride recited their vows

to defend their country; "till death
do us part" in this day and age ought to

be for growing old after lives of bliss,
not as casualties on the battlefield

of their homeland, where they should build
a marital home and not a bunker.

the newlyweds received their benediction
and rifles, and locked their arms

with the safety catch. the loaded
question is whether their spending the rest

of their lives together can be measured
in decades instead, tagged as happy ending

Bobby Z (USA)
Bobby Zielinski aka Bobby "Z" the 81 year old war Veteran, cancer survivor, recovering alcoholic, and original Jersey City 50's (high school dropout) bad boy.
E: biz17alty@verizon.net

THE UKRAINE DREAM

The Ukraine Dream, with streets once paved with gold,
now filled with bombed out bldg's and military detours.
the Dream has now been put on hold.

Once dreaming of greatness, and awaiting just rewards,
which Putin has attempted to vanquish, will once again be restored.

Their family's have left, and now safely over the border,
while they remain to fight, wondering if they will ever again,
be with their wife's, son's or daughters.

Bullets flying, bombs exploding, guided missiles in the air,
Zelensky taunting Putin, come and get us,
come and get us, because were going nowhere,

The will to succeed, has not been lost thru the year
we shall fight for our freedom, and never have any fears.

No shortage of role models, our youth have many hero's to look up to,
they have replaced their dreams, with bearing arms,
willing to sacrifice for you, you & you.

Putin has made a mistake, and has found out, but its to late,
that it's not the size of the dog, but the size of the fight in the dog,
I guess he took the bait.

It's without a doubt, that Pres Zelensky has courage,of the highest degree,
has nightly dreams about the Ukraine Dream, and that Ukraine,
will once again become *FREE*.

The dream once again shall rise, once many changes are made,
we shall once again return to the greatness of yesterday, and we will never again be dismayed.

John Davis (USA)
John lives on an island in Washington state. He is a poet, author and polio survivor, and his work has appeared in a number of magazines and journals.
E: jhdutah@gmail.com

NOT A NIGHT OF CEASE FIRE

They cannot bury the dead, they cannot
when booms and blasts flatten the buses,
flatten the streets when air raid sirens blast
the town when bombs bombast a smoke and ash.
So sharp the snipers, the dead-eye dicks
whose trigger fingers find a being, aim,
release and aim again, another click
another clack just a being, no name.
Hidden from shelling inside the basement,
surrogate newborns gurgle and coo,
cuddle with nannies. Parents from London and Kent
from Beijing and Bahrain wait for a breakthrough.
Barrages burst while nannies tie on bibs,
hug the babies, bounce them on their laps.

Smeetha Bhoumik (INDIA)
Smeetha lives in Mumbai. She is a poet, artist, editor and founder of Women Empowered - India (WE) - a literary community with poetry at its heart.
E: smeethabhoumik@gmail.com

FLOW TOWARDS PEACE

In the rise and fall
      Trough, crest and
           Flow
Of numerous thoughts

Where terrains and visions unite,
Are scenes of Ukraine -
Vistas of wonder
Yet under siege and prone, vulnerable

Like richly endowed forests
Of beauteous promise.
      Submerged in lived hours now, so
Laborious and painstaking.

To Ukraine are flowing
Our thoughts, our prayers and
All the hope for
Peaceful tomorrows

As enchanted waters of the
Dnieper, Dniester, Southern Buh
And Siversky Donets
Fill the land with eternal magic:

Impervious as rivers are to
The follies and misadventures
Of an imperfect humanity!
Struggling to survive.

Cynthia Atkin (USA)
Based in Virginia, Cynthia worked as the assistant director for the Poetry Society of America. She is the author of two books, and her work has appeared in journals and anthologies worldwide.
E: Cynthia.atkins1@gmail.com
W: www.cynthiaatkins.com

THE LAST CRICKET STANDING
No wind is too cold for lovers—Ukranian Proverb

Are you the tiny creature taking up
the entire night skies? — Our private
garage band, teasing us with longing? —
    As if silence were a dance
on a magnetic field. Lyrical, diaphanous creature,
you're the essence of all the good sounds—
dishes clanking, saxophones, laughter.
This trill is the opposite of a tea kettle
    shrieking. Not at all the siren's pitch
of warning just before a building
is level bombed. The opposite of a gunshot—
    The endless echo. You're the hieroglyphs
we work to understand. No misgivings, prick-spur
of our pride, the sandbags buff March winds.
You are the old ladies whispering
    under kitchen lights. The earworm
singing to pyjama-bottomed teen boys,
tapping chewed-off pencils on schoolbooks.
You are pulsing in the hips of the couple
    f***ing in the next room—
next room to the next room of the dead.
From the last blooms of August, sunflowers rise
    from the ashes of our ancestors.
The women are lighting *Shabbos* candles
with Molotov Cocktails—A baby is passed to arms
on a train. Looking for the sound of peace
in a song—breathing, the whole world is in on it.

Maria Editha Garma-Respicio (HONG KONG / PHILIPPINES)
Maria has been working in Hong Kong for almost two decades. She is a member of various poetry platforms, and a regular contributor to international poetry publications.
E: garmaedith8@gmail.com
FB: @editha.g.respicio

WAKE-UP

young and old are running away
from the rampant destruction
of their once sanctuary
but now a war zone
they are pleading
crying for peace and justice
to their aggressor to wake up
that avarice and covetousness
be turned to compassion
stop the shedding of blood
their lives matter
just like you

wake-up
to the one in power
all conflicts can be resolved
in a diplomatic way
wake-up before it's over
don't act as if you owned the world
you're just the steward
your life is temporal
you'll soon meet your demise
so change your course journey
listen to your convictions
bury your crooked ideologies
before bad karma
follows you

Binod Dawadi (NEPAL)
Binod lives in Kathmandu. He has completed his Master's Degree, majoring in English. His poetry and stories can be seen in a large number of publications worldwide.
E: vinoddawadi9@gmail.com

WAR IN UKRAINE

Wars are going on,
People are killed,
World can't stop these wars,
Ukraine you just hold the hands and bear that,
World is your body guard don't worry,

Don't lose your hope,
Don't get afraid and sad,
War will finish one day,
Don't worry Ukraine,
These war can't heal you we are in your support.

Peace

Russia stop the war,
In the Ukraine,
Stop to kill the life,
Why you are playing the terrific games,
Stop these wars and bring peace,
In the world,
Live happily by helping each other,

By loving and caring each other,
Russia Ukraine is your neighbourhood,
Why you are attacking there,
Stop the wars and bring peace,
Peace is needed to live in a happy life,
Know the importance of the peace,
Stop the war, Russia.

Jose Manoj Mathews T (INDIA)
Jose is based in Kochi and is an English teacher. He writes poetry in both English and Malayalam, and has had a few of his poems published.
E: mathewstjosemanoj@gmail.com

UNKNOWN ANSWERS

Who is right and who's wrong?
That is not the question now.
Who is alive, who are dead
This is unknown to us now.
Bombs explode, and shells shatter and
Kill a lot of kids and moms.
You are bombing you are killing
You don't know the taste of death.
You sit in a big building and
It is far away you see.
Come to this place watch dead people
Don't you have a family?
They are safe and secured in a
Big palace in your country.
You are strong and you have soldiers
They are killing children now
Who could stop this, who can save them?

No one knows the answer now.

Ivana Radojičić (SERBIA)
Ivana lives and works Belgrade. She is the author of one novel, editor of one poetry book, and has been published in a large number of national and international magazines.
E: gorodecki.a@gmail.com
Instagram: @ivana_radojicic_art

A DANDELION?

Tiny delicate dandelion
Opening himself to the world,
Slowly.
Shy.
Everything is so new.
The sun warmth on his yellow petals,
The bees buzzing over the meadow,
His cheeks blushing at a look of a beautiful daisy next to him.

He started waking up early to catch dew
To clean his leaves and beautiful yellow crown.
To be at his best when his lady wakes up.

They would look at the Sun together,
Then at the stars during night.
He would put his leaves around her when she felt cold.

One day,
Scared animals started running away.
"What is happening? Why are you so afraid?"
"Big metal animals are coming."

Dandelion was afraid.
Daisy was crying.
Earth was shaking.
Giant metal caterpillar was going straight towards them
Grinding the ground.

Dandelion grabbed his daisy and laid flat on the ground.
Dirt was everywhere.
Grass was screaming while being slaughtered.
But he was holding his love as hard as he could.

There was not much left
Of once happy and green meadow.
Innocent flowers were dead.
Grass was mixed with pieces of dirt.

Only dandelion and his daisy
Holding leaves.
Heads high
Crying at the Sun.

Tricia Lloyd Waller (ENGLAND)
Tricia lives on the boarder of North London and Hertfordshire. She volunteers with early years readers at her local library, and has recently had some of her work published.
E: serendipity52@hotmail.com
FB: @Tricia Lloyd Waller
Instagram: @lilyofaday
Twitter: @TriciaJean44

IT IS NOT ENOUGH

It is not enough!
He turns to avoid looking at her crumpled face.
The cans, the cuddly toys, the cash.
It is not enough he repeats.
I must go and fight!

Turning back he faces his Ukrainian Mother.
It is not enough!
He repeats through teary eyes
to send things.
I must go and fight!

But you my son are not Ukrainian.
born here in this English town.
But you my Mother are he whispers
lowering his eyes he repeats
I must go and fight!

And in the bright morning sunshine
her broken heart swells with pride
as she embraces
her beloved and only son
probably for the very last time.

Ed Ruzicka (USA)
Ed is an occupational therapist based in Louisiana. He has had two books published, and has been featured in a large number of journals and anthologies.
E: edzekezone@gmail.com
W: www.edrpoet.com/poems

KIEV

I have been 2x vaccinated against the shingles
an affliction commercials show
as lava crackling on top of skin.
Nerve endings go haywire.
I feel safer now as I go
room to room at the hospital
where rashes and lesions
routinely write themselves into
the parchment skin of our elderly.

Of course, my safety does nothing
for anyone bunkering
in the subways of Kiev
as Russia gives it another
deep dive into history and a lesson
on the marvels of modern war-craft
so Putin can have his triumph
of fallen apartments, of limbs ripped from bodies.

Brick and mortar cough as they rise
and tumble, topsy-turvy, orchestrated
by what music of decimation
is created at the tip of missile.
There now is the little girl
in her inadequate sweater
who wanders out of rubble.
She will need a new mother.

Instead she finds a dusty kitten.
Over and over, in passionate whispers,
the girl promises to be the kitten's protector.
I am safe and I am trying to stay safe.
In the worst of times eyes turn to stone
and March is more cruel than kind.

Igor Pop Trajkov (NORTH MACEDONIA)
Based in Skopje, Igor is a prolific writer across all genres of literature, including poetry, theory and journalism. Published widely, his work has been translated into many languages.
E: igorpoptrajkov@yahoo.com
FB: @Igor Pop Trajkov(Luka)

CONTINUATION

In high spirits your all was, the first time I
saw you. Dressed in that dark suit with
dark shirt, and dark scarf, all suits well
on your darkened face, on your rejuvenated
tan were your eyes searching for nothing
while acquiring everything.
It was in that theatre beneath the ground
that you were visiting to be influencing
everything against the dictatorships
your ancestors were experiencing.

You were wearing those same clothes
but so many different reactions you
caused for different malevolencies
while we were talking about so many
things we had in common, as evil was
well-known for us both.

Ordinariness creates the big evil, so
nobody pays attention to it, it just
grows everywhere poor fugitives go
— your parents Jews from Ukraine were
in the station, in the Mediterranean
landscape, God gave them you
who was sleeping in the cheap
hotels of the East, speaking
against everything causing trouble
to human- that poorest thing.

I thought your origin was from
Croatia, because there is a big
d.o.p. with your family name
I didn't know all with your family
name were Jews, I couldn't Google
you then, then there was no Internet.

I actually knew nothing of you then

knowing nothing of everything
so you told me, like to your neighbour ...

I wonder what you thought of me then
we laughed, we had so much fun
I tend to believe you sensed I am
against same things you were then
you saw that moor in my pupils.
But I know we with the moor are
more, our army is big as human kind
can be when left sparkling with its
virtue, as Virgil's boy in its infant storm.

I know what you were doing was not
in vain, many appreciate the knight
when they see he is alone but strong
to the bone, all those poor belong
to him only, their path is cruel, bold
so bloody, as honesty only can be.
Where are your dark clothes now-
you monk? Do you still do everything?
You know what? You'll gonna win!

Mantas Stočkus (MALTA / LITHUANIA)
Originally from Lithuania, Mantas has an MA in Modern & Contemporary Literature and Criticism. His writing has appeared in various print and digital publications.
E: stockus.mantas@gmail.com

ON A HIGHWAY

A man stands in the middle of the highway. Over a month ago it was full of cars and trucks ebbing and flowing from and to the capital. But now, even a snail can have the time to pass to another side. The site of the smoke at the end of the horizon – stretching through the sky – recalls him the times when he was a student. Almost a month ago. And yet, so distant as if hidden in the history books about the origins of Ukraine itself. Behind the trunk, lays his best friend. He also wanted to be a painter. Everyone thought of him highly at the university: half-bombed and half-burned building where instead of youthful voices, the wind howls at nights. The first appears in the distance. Ten minutes. The man takes the snail and joins the others, resting by the side of the highway. Soon, more of those things will rise from the smoke as if from the hell itself. Another one with a flag on its back – dragging the red line as a sign of intention – crops up. None of the group look back at the places where they all grew up and hoped for a better future. The third and the fourth pop out simultaneously. Five minutes. And another one. His friend tells a joke about their dreams. They all laugh. Three minutes. Someone lights a cigarette. Maybe the last one of the day... One minute.

Jyotirmaya Thakur (ENGLAND / INDIA)
Jyotirmaya is an internationally renowned poet and writer. She has published 25 books, and her work has been featured in more than 500 anthologies and magazines worldwide.
E: jyotirmaya.thakur@gmail.com
FB: @jyotirmaya.thakur

WAR VICTIMS
On Russian invasion of Ukraine

She was on a journey to unknown destiny
War had torn her family apart
Searching for safety of survival
Her tottering baby steps took the plunge
Right beside her mother holding hands
Innocently trusting the strangers smiles
Over the harsh territories and landscapes
To the fringed future of feathers
Fluttering within the frames of another
Unmarked lagoons of sweltering sweats
Tossing the pearls of priceless tears
The poverty and pains of migration
Melting into wavering world of realisation
Pulchritude of foreigners procreation
In temporary shelters of warm consolation
Despite agonies in endurance
Leaving abundance of life for adversity
Continuous endeavours of pacifists
Against utmost floundering falsities
Searching for rehabilitation and sanity
It is the tragic tales of nothingness
A transitory route of togetherness
In the galvanised graves of geography
Barbaric tactics to kill and plunder
Bestial crimes for enemies to surrender
Dictators fight to increase their territory
Fate of war children destroyed perpetually.

Victoria Walker (ENGLAND)

Based in Torquay, Victoria works on a dementia unit, and has a great love for helping others. She has recently signed a publishing contract for a book she has written on the subject of poems about life.
E: vic0409@live.co.uk

AWAY FROM HOME!

"Where are we going mother? Do you know? Why are we out in the freezing snow?"
"Somewhere safe, my mother replied. To quiet nights and calmer skies."
"Mother what has happened to our friend's house, it's cracked in half and falling down!?"
"War is upon us my mother replied, with a shaky voice and tears in her eyes. We are not safe now, we have to leave. Wiping tears on the fold of her sleeve"
"But Mother this is our home, I said. What did we do to cause this fight. Why are they trying to destroy our homes in the dead of night?"
"My mother looked at me and said, we did nothing my child. We made our home, lived in peace and left others alone."
"Sometimes peace is not enough, ambition of others consumes the love."
"Mother what of our family, my friends and home?" How will we move these heavy stones?"
" My mother looked at me and said. My dear child, you are my world, I'll hold you tight in this bitter cold, it breaks my heart for you to see, how cruel this world can truly be!"

Tony Frisby (ENGLAND)
Tony graduated from Brunel with an MA in Modern Literature, and subsequently did a PhD in Irish Poetry. He is the author of five poetry collections.
E: macfirbisig@gmail.com
FB: @tony.frisby.1

UNIMAGINABLE!
'All my pretty ones? Did you say all? What, all my pretty chickens and their dam at one fell swoop?' Macbeth Act iv scene iii

Unimaginable, beyond insane; and yet
even as Ukrainian babies are blown to bloody pieces
in this latest excursion into the nightmare realms of conflict,
there exists a room where the etiquette of War
is, once again, being discussed and decided upon.

Perhaps it's a large stateroom in a secluded mansion;
somewhere quiet and peaceful, somewhere
delegates won't be distracted by the ululations
of grieving parents; somewhere
corporate Cadillacs, armoured Bentleys

and military personnel carriers
won't be hindered by protesters,
as they sweep majestically
from the real world of body-counts
to that unimaginable room,

where the etiquette of Wars is decided
by well-groomed arms-dealers, be-medalled Generals,
power-mad politicians and crazed zealots
negotiating the tricky rules of collateral damage
while sipping goblets of blood-red wine.

*But who speaks for the babies as the war-mongers
brew their lethal concoction of words, designed solely
to excuse the dismembered bodies
of all our pretty chickens and their* dam?
Saws, Adages and well-worn Clichés

Once again, our tortured world has turned
upon a murderous axis and, once again,
I find myself scrabbling amongst my Mother's hoard
of well-worn clichés to help me deal
with these Banshee times.

And sometimes it's only the simplest of adages
- a saying as old as time and already drenched in tears-
that can help me chew what I cannot stomach in the raw;
a saw, that like a parent's quiet whisperings,
mighty offer refuge in the dark.

And so I wrap myself in childhoods comfort blankets;
deal with trauma as if a mantra
could make it bearable; as if her treasured, treasure-store
of worn-out motes could numb the pain
or cauterise my fears.

It's the only way I can manage;
"At least it was quick.",
finding something positive to say
about an elderly neighbour shuffling off
to the sound of fiddles at an Irish wake.

But these newest deaths are different;
they're not mundane deaths; not normal deaths;
not growing old deaths but deaths in Ukraine,
deaths so grim, so bloody unfair, so f***ing, f***ing cruel,
so heedless of all the pretty children and their parents

that the bared, primal grimace of a cornered animal
shapes my lips and from the safe haven
of a Mother's apron this shivering boy-man
screams at the adult world
through sepulchred, tombstone teeth.

Geoff Ward (REPUBLIC OF IRELAND / ENGLAND)
Geoff is a writer, poet, musician, singer-songwriter and journalist, who lives near Co. Cork. With an MA and BA (Hons) degrees in literature, he is also a book editor and writing tutor.
E: gjohnward@btopenworld.com

I MIGHT GO BAREFOOT ON THE RECEIVING EARTH

I might go barefoot on the receiving earth
wash in the waters of the spangled sun-lake
fill my eyes with the sky at dawn and sunset
sail with the mandrake moon on a tide of stars

I might sit among the rocks and watch the sea
listen well as the breeze whispers its secrets
dream on clouds that cluster to the mountain peak
tend a winter hearth for my lover's return

I might speak of spirit with the ancient stones
chase the headlong streams from crag to tumbling shore
sigh with the listless leaves of moody autumn
revel in the raindrop that begirds the storm

And even if my heart might slow relentless time
still I must share the burden of sorrowful souls

Susie James (USA)
Susie lives in Iowa. She is, by education, a classical pianist. Her poetry has been published in journals and magazines worldwide, and in several anthologies.
E: suzyclaire52@gmail.com

EXODUS UKRAINE

The road out of town is littered,
a jacket, a pink plastic comb,
churned up mud and white thickets of dead grasses,
a blue scarf caught on a twig.
The river of suffering flows under a pewter sky.
The air smells of gunpowder.

A fox trots along the hedge row.
Another sits waiting in the clearing.
They meet, touch noses, and glance over.
The walkers hold the hands of children,
speak quietly, keep moving.
The grey shadows vanish into dry grasses,
leaving only a ripple. An owl cries.

Carol Seitchik (USA)
Carol is based in Massachusetts. She is the author of one poetry collection, and her poems have been published in a number of other international anthologies and journals.
E: carolsei@comcast.net

THE WAY WE THINK

"God lives in the chaos – in the things that are not quite what you expected them to be ..." Michael Stipe, artist.

Books are bundled on my desk
and wedged in between
small plastic flags I have collected
from different countries
that fly from car windows
or balconies, sold in curio shops
and further askance
up the wall, upon the ceiling
where the old capped-off
light fixture once was
a spider rushes across
in its spiderly way
leaving no markings on its journey
its passage of life, so fragile
even preposterous in its attempt
at destination, even arbitrary
even as spiders when removed
from building their webs
even days later finish
where they had left off
those protectors of the homeland
to repel the enemy
and what are boundaries for
like so many worlds
where civilians take up guns
how the fury attaches
and we who stand by
dream-like, where nothing
is quite fastened down
to our own delicate web
perpetually unfinished
in its haphazard way and
as the Buddha said
in his dharma wisdom
nothing will happen

the way
we think.

Abdumominov Abdulloh (UZBEKISTAN).
Abdumominov is a 13 year-old poet from Tashkent. He started writing when he was ten years-old and has already has work published internationally.
E: abdumominovabdulloh470@gmail.com

PEACE

May there always be peace,
Let there be no war.
May our country be beautiful,
Rejoice, our people.
Wherever you go, always,
Do good to you.
They say that even the ancestors,
The near future is you.

Always in our country,
It's a wedding, it's a spectacle.
Tulips on the hill,
Come on guys.

We celebrate,
Now you guys.
In our independent hands
When we live happily.

William R Stoddart (USA)
Based in Southwestern Pennsylvania, William is a Pushcart nominated poet and fiction writer. His work has appeared in a large number of magazines and journals.
E: bill_stoddart@yahoo.com

TWO-HEADED EAGLE

Two-headed eagle
eyes its able prey,
living where might makes right.

Targets in sight,
itching for another fray,
the eagle in flight.

Turning blue skies to night,
logic a blind shade of gray,
living where might makes right.

The eagle with ravenous sight,
collateral to hold or slay?
The eagle in flight.

Damage surveyed at first light,
the eagle is here to stay,
living where might makes right.

Please ignore the friendly fire,
oily incense from the pyre,
two-headed eagle,
living where might makes right.

Christine Aurelio (HONG KONG / PHILIPPINES)
Originally from Capiz in the Philippines, Christine works as a domestic worker in Hong Kong. She writes to be heard, not to compete.
E: prophetetine@gmail.com
FB: @kat.sommers.96
Instagram: @christineaurelio1

LISTEN TO THEM

Blankets and sleeping bags to take
Homes gone was the worst dream to awake
Going here and there to hide with fear
A voice in prayer under the clouds appear

A gray smoke from a burning house
Women in bandage and bloody blouse
An innocent kid running with a toy
Words of sadness, humanity destroy

The dying dreams of young and old
Kindness to share and peace are gold
Feed our crying sisters and brothers
Love and care to one another

Soldiers risking their own life
To protect family from dangerous strife
Respect and solidarity to the nation
Different story of sorrow and inspiration

Listen to them for they are in pain
A helping hand for their strength to gain
Plead for safety and to end the blooded sword
For justice and people's dignity to stack in cord

Til Kumari Sharma (NEPAL)
Also known as Pushpa, Til has published over 6000 poems and 180 essays and other literary works, and is currently doing a PhD in English Literature from Singhania University, India.
E: authortilkumarisharma@gmail.com

PLEASE, PAUSE WAR

Bring peace and prosperity to have kindness in human world.
The mourning and killing harm both sides of world.
Ukraine is in ditch now it bears the tears and death.
When grave is one of both countries, why need the war?
Kind humanity deals the worth and peace.
Oh, Power, give birth to peace and revive the humanity.
The world is mourning to destruction and death caused by battle of Russia and Ukraine.
Hope for peace and prosperity with great civilization.

Suchismita Ghoshal (INDIA)
Suchismita hails from West Bengal. She is an widely published author and bilingual poet, spoken word poet and professional writer, and has been invited to many international festivals and events.
E: storytellersuchismita@gmail.com
E: ghoshalsuchismita019@gmail.com

UKRAINE, MY DEAR

Paranoia hitting my head
As I find myself trembling ...
The terrors coming from the pictures of war.
Ukraine, my dear, are you able to breathe,
The air contains poisons of war-lovers and bombs;
Trading is a hotspot as people's lives are being sold.
Ravages of time or ravages of ego?
What should we consider this devastating trepidation?
Are we even in the situation to articulate anything?
Ukraine, my dear, my heart cries, everyday at a stretch,
Compassion won't work anymore which I know
And you are wombing pain and blood, sobs and hurts, dead bodies and cremation, lost homes and peace;
I know all of it through the sensation of my soul.
The dirty obsession of power-possession
Should end or else, the universe won't mercy at all!
Ukraine, my dear, we are with you
Lighting up a lamp everyday for the better days to arrive!

Finola Scott (SCOTLAND)
Based in Glasgow, Finola is a proud grandmother. Her poems are published widely.
E: finolascott@yahoo.com
FB: @Finola Scott Poems

WHERE'S DOLLY?

Worried she looks everywhere,
spots silly Teddy hiding under
the pillow. But Dolly isn't there.
Mummy said to pick one toy, but
she struggles to leave cuddly pals.
She can't ask Daddy. He hunts,
muttering. Papers, they're here.
Passports, must find them. Must.
The noise again, that horrid monster
howling. It really scares Dolly.
Mummy is packing. Holiday!
Mummy did talk about shells.
She must tell Dolly. The seaside,
not down in the inky underground.

If only those nasty noises would stop.

Louis Faber (USA)
Based in Florida, Louis is of Lithuanian, Scottish, Irish, English and German heritage. His work has been published internationally.
E: lfaberfl@outlook.com

FOR THEM, FOR US ALL

We sit huddled together
knowing what is to come.
Our souls are crushed
by the collapse of homes,
schools and hospitals.
Our hearts are pierced
by the shrapnel that tears
through families, bodies
torn by the ravages
of a war wholly unprovoked.
Our eyes are blinded
by the tears of families
not knowing, fearing to know.
And yet our hope is kindled
by the ferocious spirit
of a young woman taking
up arms, an old man
hobbling to the front
desperate to protect
the freedoms that we
all too often take for granted.

John Notley (THAILAND / ENGLAND)
John was a travel agent for 40 years. Now retired, he spends much of his time in Thailand where he writes short stories and poetry.
E: john.notley@gmail.com

WORDS NOT WAR

The hounds of war have yet again
been loosed upon another's soil.
While nations watch them powerless
shake their heads, with fear recoil.

Bombs and rockets from the heavens
take their toll on all below
Splitting families, causing sorrow
how much grief we'll never know.

While families flee ensuring safety
in nearby cities unknown to them
Their homes destroyed, reduced to rubble,
their lives disrupted never to return again?

One man's vision from his bunker
sees an empire within his grasp.
His chance to make a new world order
to turn the clock to glories past.

Will this madness ever finish
will God's word at last prevail.
Will men ever learn to live in peace
using words not wars, or fail?

Colette Tennant (USA)
Colette is an English professor based in Oregon. She has published two books of poetry, and her poems have been included in various local and international journals.
E: CTennant@corban.edu
FB: @colette.tennant

RISKY

Streets filled with rubble,
a bombed maternity hospital, pregnant women
bloodied, lying on gurneys in a swirl of confusion,
Sasha, a baby goat with broken front legs,
trying to nurse a vet tech's ear.
Her owner promised she'd return for her
because she loves her.

We watch the news from Ukraine –
refugees bundled against late-winter cold.
In between these stories, news channels
run commercials for various cures –
Nucala for severe asthma sounds great,
but it might cause shingles.
Trelegy treats COPD yet increases
the risk of thrush, pneumonia
and osteoporosis.
Farxiga, for chronic kidney disease,
might lead to dehydration, fainting, weakness,
genital redness and swelling, and hypoglycaemia.

It's a tricky balance,
the cure and its reaction, so
military experts sit with newscasters,
their hands folded on the studio table.
They discuss various scenarios
for how to help Ukraine, each one
peppered with what ifs.
One possible cure – establish a no-fly zone
unless Putin reacts with chemical weapons.
Supply warplanes to the Ukrainians,
order an airstrike on that 40-mile-long convoy,
but any of those moves might start World War III.
It's a terrible quandary,
this war we watch between commercials –
trying to find a remedy for this devastation,
knowing the reaction may be awful.

Xe M. Sánchez (SPAIN)
Xe is an anthropologist Based in the Principality of Asturias. He received his PhD in History, and has published seven books in the Asturian language.
E: sanchez.xe.m@gmail.com

IN THE DEBRIS OF MARIUPOL

I found over a sheet of paper
these anonymous words
in the smoking debris
of Mariupol:
the poors
never win the wars,
not even when they win them.
Maybe these words
will not appear,
the next century,
in the future History books
(because History
forget the poor
and because it is poetry).

Nancy Byrne Iannucci (USA)
Nancy is a teacher, woodland roamer, and widely published poet from New York. She is the author of two chapbooks, and her work can be seen in a large number of magazines and journals
E: nancybyrneiannucci@gmail.com
W: www.nancybyrneiannucci.com

I THOUGHT ABOUT MY TWO STUDENTS

I took the same path in the morning-
woke up to find my cat lying in sunbeams,
got dressed, had breakfast, prepped
before my nine o'clock class,

then I heard the chainsaw,
cutting through Thursday's route
sending ice floating in lily pads
down Poestenkill Creek.

I could see it all from my window
driving to work,
listening to bombs on the radio,
"listening to bombs on the radio",

echoing old sounds of the twentieth century.
I put on *Stand or Fall* by The Fixx
and thought, "how the hell
can I continue my classes

on the Protestant Reformation?"
My plan was to have them assess Cranach,
Law and Gospel and Martin Luther's 95 Theses.
How can I go through with this now?

Crying parents tell their children
if you survive don't do as we did.
I thought about my two students
from Lithuania and the Ukraine,

Ugne and Yaryna,
roaming this quiet N.Y, boarding school
like Stoics, consumed by Putin
and the safety of their families back home.

I decided to keep Luther's 95 Theses
nailed to the Wittenberg church door.

Impromptu teaching has always terrified me,
but what right do I have to feel this way now,

when red-lit metal boxes
are jamming Kyiv highways
in a desperate attempt to flee the city.
What do I know about fear?

Ugne and Yaryna forced a good morning smile.
I stared at the class for a painful moment,
then nailed Putin to the whiteboard.
Oh! Their faces! Their Munch faces!

I tried to answer all their questions,
giving Ugne and Yaryna a moment to speak,
to cry, to be consoled by their classmates,
many of whom had not heard what had happened

until now.

Fiona Owen (WALES)
Based in Anglesey, Fiona teaches for the Open University. She has had four poetry collections published, and her writing can be found in a variety of journals, magazines and anthologies.
E: fionaowen@btinternet.com
W: www.rhwng.com

SELFIES FOR PEACE
Response to Wanda Garner's film 'Real Women of the World', written during Putin's invasion of Ukraine, March 2022

For Eileen

They carried her over rubble on a stretcher,
her belly huge with imminent child,
the bombed-out maternity hospital

behind her in splinters, dazed women,
children, doctors, nurses staggering
out of its smoking shell.

Now, as I watch each woman's face in the film
slide past, standing for peace, for solidarity,
each selfie a small act of resistance, an appeal

against what is here again, another man's war,
your face appears, friend over decades, closely
interwoven into my own life's fabric

and I picture us, two women of Wales, as them,
on a crowded platform somewhere: I'm pushing
through the throng, everyone desperate, everyone

pushing, when I glimpse you, in your dog-walking fleece,
your blonde bob, created in peacetime, awry. Shouting
across the many heads your name, your name, I start

swimming, it feels, against an impossible current
as the one train blows its whistle to leave.

In this story, the woman safely births her baby
and you hear me over the hubbub, turn, our eyes
meet, arms stretch, hands reach, grasp, hold on

past happy endings or make-do starts to where
we're all part of what is or may be, each life

a legacy of hope, of *keep trying*, of *never give up* on the pregnant potentials for peace.

Djehane Hassouna (USA)
Based in Pennsylvania, Djehane grew up a few steps away from the Egyptian pyramids. At 62 years-old, she earned her PhD and, at the age of 76, published her first book.
E: djehane@gmail.com
W: www.djehane-poetry.com
FB: @DjehanePoetry
Instagram:@ DjehanePoetry
Twitter:@DjehanePoetry

WHAT IS WAR?

War is tears; war is fear;
War is error; war is terror;
War is pain and suffering for all.
War is a man-made hell.
War is the end of civilization.
War is living by the law of the jungle.
War is never victory but a constant defeat.
War is a stain on the face of History.
War is rewriting humanity in blood and tears.
War is ratified vandalism, a doomed legacy.
War is a blot on the conscience of Man.
War drives us back to the Stone Age.
Although war is far away,
I can hear the rumbling of explosions,
The detonations of grenades and missiles;
While people are dying for no reason,
I can see flames engulfing the horizon,
I can feel the horror of a blood bath:
It all reverberates into my existence.
I bid adieu to a peaceful conscience ...

Tatiana Gritsan-Chonka (UKRAINE)
Tetyana lives in Transcarpathia, She is the author of 11 collections of poetry, a novel, and the co-author of 57 Ukrainian and international anthologies and almanacs.
E: tet-a-tetana@ukr.net

UNTITLED

Water is Spring, Peace.
That melting, that - not quilting – Assumption ...
When the Creator bends to walk with our heads,
When on our imaginary title there is only one stomping ground - *Cohan*.
Not everything becomes clean, when we are wearing a *yarb*,
Like a beaten apple ...
The meal is over. Not all are finished,
not all merchants want to be taken to sin.
Not everyone is a craftsman who wears more,
Not the last one...
The eyes have remained - the eyesight of the sky, of purity,
There is still a love affair,
Spring, water, and you,
That young boy with songs,
That shining candle with books,
Where all the world flies,
Where we will grow up to a stitch together ...
We are all now on *Ti* in the dreamy structure.

Jake Cosmos Aller (SOUTH KOREA / USA)
Former Foreign Service Officer, (US Diplomat), Jake lives in South Korea. He has been writing poetry and short stories for decades, and has had work published in over 25 literary journals.
E: authorjakecosmosaller@gmail.com
W: www.theworldaccordingtocosmos.com

WHEN RUSSIA INVADED UKRAINE

When Russia invaded Ukraine
The bombs killed thousands.

When Russia invaded Ukraine
The Ukrainian people stood up.

When Russia invaded Ukraine
Putin misunderestimated Zelensky,

When Russia invaded Ukraine
Putin thought Biden would do nothing.

When Russia invaded Ukraine
NATO was reborn.

When Russia invaded Ukraine
The Russian people turned on Putin.

When Russia invaded Ukraine
The sanctions wiped out billions of his wealth.

When Russia invaded Ukraine
The world came together demanding NO MORE WARS.

When Russia invaded Ukraine
He wished his puppet, Trump, was still president

Sunayna Pal (USA)
Born India, Sunayna now resides in Maryland. Her poetry is published extensively in international journals and anthologies.
E: sunayna.pal@gmail.com
W: www. sunaynapal.com
FB: @LearningAboutSindh

DARK CLOUDS HAVE COME

It hasn't rained here - yet,
but the clouds have come.
Dark clouds that swallowed the sun
have painted the sky - black.

Loud, threatening thunder
with sparks everywhere
summoning the dark rain.

Hopeless prayer
subdued by the storm
lightens the omen
but it will rain.

The earth will bear
yet another torrent,
and be drenched.

Suzanne Newman (ENGLAND)
Suzanne lives in the Midlands. She has been writing poetry since 2018, and finds it cathartic following a harsh battle with a rare, aggressive form of cancer, and subsequent clinical depression.
FB: @snewmanpoetry

I CAN'T DO THIS ALONE

I'm breaking. "I can't do this alone!"
I yell, as I stumble down life's long, hard road,
Back's buckling under this trial's heavy load,
Whilst my weary heart beats weakly … fractured and slow.

I collapse down on my woeful knees,
Head's pounding with stress … can't seem to find peace,
Angst is trapped and pacing, searching for a release,
And stomach's unsettled, like a cross swarm of bees.

Intense grief's made me feel so sick,
Whilst depression has snared me within its dark pit,
Anxiety's cobra rears, hisses and spits,
And pain's earthquake causes flesh and bone to split.

Frustration, confusion and sanity groan,
Emotions tornado to destroy peaceful home,
I cry with no strength, "I can't do this alone!",
Jesus says, "You don't have to. You're not on your own."

Sudhakar Gaidhani (INDIA)
Sudhakar's poems have been translated into several languages, and he has received many state, national and international literary prizes and awards.
E: sudhakargaidhani@gmail.com

WHITE HANDKERCHIEF
Translated from Marathi by Dr. OmBiyani

The flesh may tire
but the mind does not
The mind being tired
no war can be fought

Often the scabbards,
brave onlookers,
dangling about the fighters' waists,
observe the clashing and sparking of swords
but not the return of the steel to its home.
And no one can rightly tell
which broken wrist grappled which hilt
whether of Russia or of Ukraine.

But war is war, it doesn't cease
no one has a plain white handkerchief,
and the war -shirts have all been
long dyed deep.

The war -wary hope
that with the captains worn out
the fighting will subside,
the missiles prod the captains
when will you start your fight?

There is no frenzy
like the frenzy of "do or die"
Alexander may conquer a hundred worlds
but oh to be a Porus.
such conquerors to defy!
So don't be caught napping
and thereby lose a fight.

A war begins in the theatre of the mind
and body assaults body, toeing the line

It's a good rule never

to start a fight,
nor to show the back
when the enemy invites

Sreekanth Kopuri (INDIA)
Based in Machilipatnam, Sreekanth is a poetry editor and Professor of English. Published widely, he has recited his poetry worldwide, including at the University of Oxford.
E: sreekanthkopuri@gmail.com
FB: @kopuri sreekanth

A NEW NORMAL
"you'll face consequences you've never seen in history."

Since *a single death*
is a tragedy,
a million battalions
slither for beyond
along a road not taken
abiding by a decree
of a cold-blooded hand
that contemplates to send
Big Boys or *Fattest men* against
the desperate flutter of doves
sedating the peoples' psyche
for a new normal
that must stoicize the earth
into an existential oneness
towards an apocalyptic preoccupation.

Elizabeth Sophia Strauss (USA)
Elizabeth lives in New York. A Broadway artist for over a decade, working on several Tony Award winning productions, she is an author, activist, producer, publisher, professor, emcee, and realtor.
E: estrauss91@gmail.com
W: www.elizabethsophiastrauss.com

UNTITLED

I am a Jewish woman proud of my culture,
Religion, identity. Who bleeds white and blue from the
Dead Sea, past the East River, and back to
The Long Island Sound. Who continues to watch her
Heritage die in Ukraine. Who learned recently her family
Perished in the Holocaust and worries as she watches
Those being murdered in the same fields again what
Will happen next. It is sobering to learn parts
Of my family lost their lives at war again

Germain Droogenbroodt (SPAIN / BELGIUM)
With over a dozen international poetry prizes, Germain is an internationally known poet, publisher and promoter of modern international poetry. He has published 15 poetry books.
E: elpoeta@point-editions.com
W: www.point-editions.com

WAR IN UKRAINE

The almond trees are here in bloom
a delight to the eye
that loves beauty.
Soon the citrus blossoms
will spread their seductive perfume,

But elsewhere rages the war
the destruction and human suffering.

No blossoms bloom there—
they suffocate in the smoke
of barbarous violence.

Dr. Alicia Minjarez Ramirez (MEXICO)
Alicia is an internationally renowned Mexican poet. Her poems have been translated into 20 languages, and published in more than 300 anthologies around the world.
E: minjarezalicia@yahoo.com

ONLY LOVE WILL PREVAIL

Only love will prevail
When there is nothing left,
When memory fades away
As scattered dust
On the wind.

Only my words will speak
Of this love
Leaving a footprint
In silence,
To posterity ...
For other times.

When my simple name
Be erased over time
And the words remain
Over withered leaves.

Only my love for you will prevail
In your skin of verse,
In your skin of rhyme,
On your prose skin ...
Beyond the eternity borders

Dr. Rehmat Changaizi (PAKISTAN)
Rehmat is a poet, writer and philosopher. He is the author of two poetry collections, editor of two others, and has been published in several international journals, magazines and anthologies.
E: drrezi@outlook.com

STANDING ALONE

Once I saw
A small star
In a secret sky,
I felt alone …
Became sad and shy,
As other stars glittered
So bright
So happily
I almost cry!

She was a beautiful Maiden
Standing alone
In the gales of Life.
Her golden hairs
Swinging toward hearth,
I could have touched them
With my fingers
Had I tried … !

Gleaming they were
Washed with her honesty.
Then …
I saw Pits in her Cheeks,
While her Eyes and Lips
Twinkled with Love
Coated with Modesty.

Alex Chornyj (CANADA)
Based in Ontario with Ukrainian heritage, he grew up performing as a Ukrainian Carpathian dancer. In the last two years he has published three poetry books and two children's adventure books.
E: alex.chornyj@ontario.ca

LIMBS ON THIS TREE

The limbs on this tree
Have strength and fortitude
Which may at times bend
But they won't break.
We as a country
Have it within us
To share this burden
As an attack on one,
Is an infringement on all
History has shown
To stiffen your resolve
When placed in a corner.
You do not acquiesce
Why this forest of ours
Through generations
Of adversity,
Has so persevered
We are a proud people
To draw from these roots
A resilient spirit.
Which keeps us buoyant
And others have listened to my call
To defend a heritage
To light that torch.
To defy with a flame
That burns in our hearts
Slava Ukraine
May we always prevail.
As here are branches
Which do not succumb
Are staunch in their resistance
To interlopers,
Of an occupation
Which we reject
In the strongest degree
We will be heard,
Not go quietly
For this is our land

Upon which we toil
Where we stand together.

Margaret Duda (USA)
Margaret lives in Pennsylvania and has had work published various magazines, journals and poetry anthologies worldwide. She is currently working on the final draft of her first novel.
E: mduda@ceinetworks.com
FB: @Margaret Duda

IF ONLY MY MOTHER WAS STILL ALIVE

I was not surprised to see that so many Hungarians
were taking in Ukrainian refugees and making sure
they had a safe, warm place to stay and plenty to eat.

As a teen, I never knew how many were coming for dinner,
but I could be sure that no one left hungry or unhappy.
First we eat, then we talk, my Hungarian mother would say.

My mother had always loved to cook and garden and we had
a basement crammed with her canning jars filled with food
grown in the garden she tended with love behind our house.

When she was ready to open her little Hungarian diner,
she chose a spot across from the local air base because
seventeen thousand airmen were hungry and lonely.

She became their surrogate mother and confidante
and the diner always bulged with airmen eating goulash
and telling her their problems as she made time to listen.

If she was still alive, she'd probably get on the first plane
to Ukraine to help the civilians hiding in basements
leave the country in safety, sending most to Hungary.

And then she would ask Zelensky and Putin to dinner.
First we eat, then we talk, she'd tell them, asking to meet
in a small restaurant which would let her cook the meal.

Chilled cherry soup with sour cream to start,
stuffed cabbage or chicken paprikash for an entrée
and for dessert, crepes stuffed with berries in thick cream.

She always felt that anything could be solved with talk
and kindness, but not if the people were hungry, convinced
it was hard to be compassionate on an empty stomach.

"Now what is the problem, boys?" she'd ask the leaders.

"You cannot kill innocent people. Have some more
of my husband's homemade wine, eat, and tell me all."

And soon they would be discussing a cease-fire and peace.
Her food and lots of empathy was all that she would need.

Andrea Carter Brown (USA)
Andrea is a writer, poet and editor living in California. She has had four collections of poetry published, and her poems have won a number of awards including from the Poetry Society of America.
E: andreacarterbrown@gmail.com
W: www.andreacarterbrown.com
FB: @Andrea Carter Brown
Twitter: @AndreaBrownPoet
Instagram: @andreabrownpoet

TO UNDERSTAND

To understand the smashing of antiquities in Palmyra,
Mosul, or the Bamiyan Buddhas, you have to understand

the revenge bombing of Dresden for Canterbury.
Go back to the Great War and try to understand

whether the German shelling of the cathedral at Reims
was accidental or deliberate. It once was hard to understand

the Crusades, Charlemagne's soldiers slaughtered by Saracens
in an obscure pass in the Pyrenees. Now it's easy to understand

eternal disputes over faith and land, the conquered,
the dispossessed seeking redress. To understand

why settlers believe they have the right to divide
ancient olive groves, you need to understand

that the Temple in Jerusalem was levelled, the land changing
hands, again and again. Go back to Rome to understand.

To Alexander. To Achilles dragging Hector's body
around the Trojan ramparts, difficult to understand,

as his father Priam watched, his widow, a spoil of war.
The hunter Ölys was laid to rest on flowers, but to understand

he was the first of our own kind, see the arrowhead buried in
his shoulder. All too believable. All too impossible to understand.

Forthcoming in her next collection *American Fraktur*.

Ermira Mitre Kokomani (USA / ALBANIA)
Formerly a teacher and humanitarian aid team leader, Ermira is poet, essayist and translator living in New Jersey. Her poetry has appeared in various international and national anthologies and journals.
E: emitre1@yahoo.com
FB: @Ermira Mitre

A UKRAINIAN LITTLE HERO

Mother,
my ears are hurting so bad,
what's that blasting noise, mother,
breaking the chirping of birds,
blocking the murmuring of waves.
We need some bee wax son,
some bee wax to save our hearing.
But let's sing a song son
Let's sing a song for the heroes.

Mother,
you're getting tired mother,
carrying me all day long,
why isn't dad with us, mother,
to hold me on his arms.
the trenches called on Dad, son,
for his body can shield this noise,
but let's sing a sacred song, son,
Let's sing a song for our heroes.

Mother,
I am freezing cold, mother
my toes are numbed as popsicles,
I can hardly see the way, mother,
my eyelashes frosted as icicles.
Let my breath snuggle them with warmth, son,
Let my body's oil melt the frenzied cold.
But let's sing our sacred song, son,
Let's sing the song of the heroes.

Mother,
my belly is hurting, mother,
it's craving for some peanut butter,
how about some jelly mother,
or maybe a piece of chocolate?
Let me rub and soften your belly, son,
let me warm and comfort it with my love.

And, let's sing our song of survival, son,
Let's sing the song of little heroes.

Elsie Isayas Calumpiano (SINGAPORE / PHILIPPINES)
Elsie is new to poetry. She works as a foreign domestic worker, and volunteers as a Team Leader for *Uplifters,* a charity organizations offering a free online courses for domestics workers in Singapore.
E: isayaselsie@gmail.com
FB: @Isayas Elsie S

BELOVED UKRAINE

Beloved country of Ukraine!
Stay strong and stand firm,
Keep on your faith and hold still
God will hear your prayers.

He send his love and miracle
To protect and shield,
The innocent children's and people
God will never leave you.

Beloved country of Ukraine!
The Patriot civilians and soldier are here,
They are fighting with a good reason
To get Peace and democracy.

Beloved country of Ukraine!
Continue to stream like a river,
Be like a sea with open spaces and freedom.
Like a sun that never stop shining and giving hope to everyone.

Wishes from our hearts
Prayers from our souls
May God blessed and bring peace and hope to your country Ukraine
And to the entire world.

Hein Min Tun (MYANMAR)
Hein Min Tun is an award winning writer and multi-published poet, in the middle of doing his Masters Degree. His work has been featured in a number of international publications.
E: Irisharold1211@gmail.com
FB: @Iris Harold

THERE WILL COME THE TIME

There will come the time
When this spell of destructions and dooms will vanish
And the joyous dawn of Peace will break;
When we, the same slaves on separate lands, will be unshackled
To caper out in the golden rays of Freedom;
And when the blowing breeze that carries the pleasant rhythms of the Song of Peace
Will float dancing over silent mountains and murmuring rivers,
Unheard of explosions and gunfires,
Unheard of Tyrants' threatening footfalls
And free of the Sounds of Oppression and Injustice.

There will come the time
When these omnipresent streams of blood will remain only in our memories,
And the prevailing sobs and the heartbreaking goodbyes we hear now
Will change into the echoes of our hearts,
And when some of us will look back on their nightmares of Today
Only to laugh away at their old jokes
With the new shape of smile that has never appeared on their faces before.
There will come the time
When the Change will rain down on us
And our Newcomers will find a different world ...

Gary Beck (USA)
Based in New York, for much of his life, Gary worked as a theatre director. He has published 34 poetry collections, 14 novels, 3 short-story collections, 1 collection of essays, and 5 books of plays.
E: garycbeck@yahoo.com
W: www.garycbeck.com
FB: @AuthorGaryBeck

NAKED AGGRESSION

The unprovoked attack
on helpless Ukraine
kills innocent civilians
as invading Russians
devastate the land.
Motivation is questionable,
revive the lost empire,
capture the food source,
exercise power,
intimidate neighbours.
Whatever the reason
the threat is constant
for unexpected escalation
that might erupt
into nuclear exchange.

John Tunaley (ENGLAND)
John lives in North Yorkshire. He's in a few writing groups, and has had work published in a number of magazines, journals and anthologies.
E: johntunaley@yahoo.co.uk

AN EARTHLY PARADISE

I dreamt I lay on the moon's wilderness
and could see on Earth the pillars of dust
by day, becoming lines of fire by night.
The churned mud was first baked to dazzling white,
then transformed ... into gardens of delight.
Beaut'ous fields were freed of loathsome blight;
and lo; precious with Pinks, pulsing with Blue-
-Greens ... an entire planet was born anew.

Offering comfort across star-pricked space;
trailing scarves of song from cloud-head to base;
I saw sky-larks flying in Magenta skies.
... ninety feet of spiralling butterflies.
The barbed war-weapons turned blunt ... rusted Titian Red ...
... Hell faded away and became Heaven instead.

Cordelia M. Hanemann (USA)
Based in North Carolina, Cordelia is a retired professor of English. She has published in numerous national and international journals, and is now working on a first novel.
E: korkimax@gmail.com

ELSEWHERE

How is it that we put off childhood
      lay aside our dolls and toys
      turn our backs on mother father home
that our toys have become weapons
      joy sticks for drone bombers
      blowing up stick figures
      and Lego houses
that gunshots sound like fireworks
      in our neighbourhood: oh say can you see
      by the dawn's early light

How is it that silence permits atrocity
      erases the wars we have made
      hides the people killed
          towns destroyed: houses hospitals schools
that a war elsewhere: texts on cell phones
      snippets on social media and passing newsfeeds
          or as in our past without pictures   without news
      without names faces lives lived and lost
      without statistics   without cost
          is no war at all

How is it that we who have no time for war
      must have our vacations
          our meals and deals
          our children's play dates
          our luncheons and teas
          our meetings and deadlines
that only ours are the lives that matter

How is it that we cannot return
      to innocence
      to unknowing what we know
      to undoing what we have done

How is it that we could perhaps do things differently

Denise Steele (SCOTLAND)
Denise is of Scottish/French heritage and lives in Glasgow. She volunteers as a teacher of English for asylum seekers and refugees. Her poetry has been published worldwide.
E: denise@cooptel.net

I AND THOU

All night, perhaps, he has planned this,
laying survival in his cheap travel bag –
vests and a toothbrush, underpants,
a paper-wrapped sandwich for lunch.

He has his warm jacket, fastened up,
his pavement shoes, a padded cap.
Do grandchildren, playing, try it for size
brim down over their laughter?

He tells the young man in camouflage –
yes, yes indeed, he wants to enlist.
Look, he will show him, undo the straps –
see, how ready I am.

The soldier's hands clasp at his back,
on his sleeve, lion rampant and the cornfield flag.
He reins, for now, a grievous response,

pays no heed to smiles in the crowd,
closely, solely, attends.

Stilled in their moment, they cross the world.

First published *The Poets' Republic*.

DeWitt Clinton (USA)
Based in Wisconsin, DeWitt Clinton taught English, Creative Writing, and World of Ideas courses for over 30 yearsy. He has had a number of collections of poetry published.
E: clintond@uww.edu
FB: @DeWitt Clinton

AT THE END OF THE WAR
(after "The End and the Beginning," Wislawa Syzmborska, 1993)

We need to do something about all the lost limbs.
Would anybody please volunteer to search
For who has lost legs, arms, faces?

We're all thirsty, yes, but does anybody know
Where we can find a brook, a creek that
Doesn't have our floating cousins?

Yes, yes, we need a morgue, but first
We must find a few dogs to tell us
Who is beneath the stones.

We know Gertrude and Maurice and maybe
Alfonse, maybe more, all have to be found.
Bandages, surely someone has some bandages.

We want to rebuild. Does anyone have a ladder?
Let's leave God out of this for awhile.
Let's start in the square, and slowly remove

What was thrown down from the sky.
Who knows how to get a weather report?
Will there be good weather for tomorrow?

Yes, that's a good idea, but we can always
Talk, there's always a lot of time for talk.
We've got such a mess.

Brooms. Everybody, find all the brooms.
Can anyone send a letter, we need to let
Someone know this has happened.

Tomorrow we can start burning our families.
Surely someone will see the smoke.
Surely someone will come.

Joralyn Fallera Mounsel (SINGAPORE / PHILIPPINES)
Joralyn found refuge in writing poetry to ease the agony of missing home and, at the same time, found her passion. She believes that writing is magical, and has contributed to few anthologies.
E : joralynmounsel@yahoo.com
FB: @Mounsel Jora lyn Fallera

DEAREST UKRAINE

Once you are one strong tree
Standing among the highest
Then selfishness thump in sudden
And blood shed the whole of your skin
For hearts of cold,
Hungry for power and distraction
Let not the bombs and guns,
Wash away thy imports
Let not faith fall ill
like how chaos flood thy being
End is not soon
For life has written your story
Lay down not by this obstacle
For death will lost its meaning
And tears will be taken for granted
Strengthen thy limbs and foundation
Though numbers were less
For had fallen hard along the battles
Thou shall not concede.
Let your flag stand tall again!
Let your name be heard again!
U-k-r-a-i-n-e!
In my prayers, you'll remain.

Kate Young (ENGLAND)
Kate is a semi-retired teacher living in Kent. She belongs to three poetry groups, which have helped and supported her. Her work has been published in a number of magazines and anthologies.
E: kateyoung12@hotmail.co.uk
Twitter: @Kateyoung12poet.

MARIUPOL

a rubble of war rolls in
marbled in crimson folds
the colour of battle,
dust on the city's tongue

oceans of bone, scraps of skin
peel from seams
of papier-mâché mural,
concrete feeble as tissue

a high-rise razed
flat as the dirtied sheet
dragged over the slump
of a once swollen belly

percussion of war resounds,
the rise and fall of power
shrapnel and shell
lodged in grey matter

curfew breaks with dawn
and with it, birdsong,
a ricochet over broken stone
a scribble of hope on a stave

Margarita Vanyova Dimitrova (BULGARIA)
Margarita is based in the ancient city of Plovdiv. She has had her work published in a number of national and international magazines and journals.
E: margovd@abv.bg

HARMONY

Quiet tenderness,
goodness
and calm,
acceptance.
With soft sun-light
you create holy following
of Divine Providence
for harmony, for peace,
for expected touch
in our vast expanse of earth.

Kathrine Yets (USA)
Kathrine lives in Wisconsin. She is a teacher and avid poet, and has published two chapbooks. Her poetry can be found in many literary magazines and anthologies.
E: iteachlitmag@gmail.com
W: www.sites.google.com/view/authorkathrineyets/home
FB: @Author-Kathrine-Yets

DEATH TOLL
Where do we begin? The rubble or our sins? ~Bastille, Pompeii.

Where to begin?
Deaths 20,000 and counting.
A butterfly lands on the rubble
of an old church with ashes
all around— a sign of hope?
Hope feels like a stone on the tongue
when there is smoke choking.
Sin fuels the fires—
a desire, a greed.
We need to do something,
people say and drink their lattes.
Meanwhile, body bags fill
and tanks drive through the streets.
Where to end?
Ukrainian soldiers sleep in empty classrooms
and wonder about tomorrow
with their rifles at their side.
All the red of the day
bleeds into dreams.

Keith Jepson (ENGLAND)
Keith lives in Shropshire. His first collection of poetry was recently published. For Keith, poetry is a cathartic process, a release, but it's also fun and a great way to creatively record the events of his life.
E: team@maxbikespr.co.uk
W: www.maxbikespr.co.uk
FB: @Max Bikes PR
Twitter: @MaxBikesPR
Instagram: @maxbikespr

UKRAINE ...

Black Sea babies born under bombs.
Slavic slaves attacking brothers, sisters, sons.
Grey Ghost Country, sunflowers suffocated by
a red dust.
Scattered to the wind, people massed and moved.
A funeral of dogs, fleeing to the west.
Kill from a distance, not when the spittle is in your
face.
Not up close.
Sovereign state suffering, annexed by the big boots
of small, distant men.
War, expressed at the end of long table. Blood on the the floor of white marble,
Splattered on columns of the madness rhetoric.
Cluster hate.
Sunflower tall and bright on scorched monochrome earth.
Dried seeds, the husk of people, sewn on the wind, drifting in their
own land.
Dispersed memories, objects, things, dreams, blood and flesh.
Hope endures in a golden field and blue sky. A line drawn in the sand
of a single line flag.
Flash and flint from a far eastern sky, with the world watching.
Who flinches first and disturbs our comfort?
Banks of men stay to protect the rivulets of a people. Another sleeping giant,
has awoken ... grumpy, angry and ill prepared at first. Restless, like
the groggy, not needed sleep of daytime.
But he is patient, and keeps a sanctioned silence behind his walls.
The Madonna of the meadows has fled west, where we are fingers
and thumbs ... tongue tied and tide. Impotent men with only the
weapon
of words.
Shadows in the Black Sea, ancient ports cut off by a cold curtain tide, immovable iron dropped in the bays.

Sandbags in the snow.
Burred in the theatre of war, what ridiculous and shameful rhetoric. The language burns with a false pride!
The Hollow Man returns, he is present at the best and worst of mankind. He is in the blackest heart and
the warmest smile. Behind all our eyes. Only our actions speak the truth.
A Zephyr of cries.
Tiny droplets of dignified blood fall in the rain.
A small boy whispers to the moon, alone, as he waits for a train to depart...
... "let it stop!"

Laura Felleman (USA)
Laura is an accountant based in Iowa. She organizes open mics at her public library, and serves on the advisory council of Iowa City Poetry. Her chapbook is due for release soon.
E: lafelleman@gmail.com
FB: @lafelleman
Instagram: @la_fell_01
Twitter: @_felleman

MY EIGHTY-YEAR-OLD MOTHER PETITIONS GOD TO ASSASSINATE PUTIN

The chemistry of the recipe suits her disposition
if left to her own stirrings
baked delicacies would have lavished our meals:
        rhubarb cream pie, rum cake, flan with caramel
        homemade granola generous with almonds
        her bread best sliced, toasted, buttered
        batches of M&Ms/peanut butter/oatmeal
        so massive we called the cookies Monster

Dutifully, she was scientist enough to serve us sensible
always three squares, routinely four groups
a drudgery she later shamelessly retired to my Father

"When did Putin turn puffy?" I'm appalled
"He's an old man," my husband matter-of-facts
but I posit Putin's body balloons
pressured by the prayers of wilful mothers
who choose to flout maternal conventions
flaunting an appetite to laden him
with all that is sticky-sweet unhealthy

Lorraine Sicelo Mangena (ZIMBABWE)
Based in Bulawayo, and studying for a career in Public Relations & Marketing Communications, Lorraine is a 21 year-old student, poet and spoken word artist.
E: loloemangena@gmail.com
FB: @Lorraine Sicelo Mangena

A LETTER TO RUSSIA

Dear Master Bullet,
You are rushing while you are exactly where you needed to be.
A kiss once betrayed the redeemer so it never defined love,
And a red rose never signified love because red was also for danger.

It was me and you,
Now it's us and war; I cannot sign up for a three-some.
Your greediness is straining the knees of my voice,
Let me hand over the microphone to the heart.

… so like a rocket ship along the highway,
Too arrogant to massage our pride,
A head on collision occupied the dance floor ;
That was the intertwining of our bullets.

Pray tell I danced to the duet,
When your bully mind kissed a blast furnace.
You wanted to paint the vacuum?
While the red sea dried up and I was sweating.

This world has turned out to be a slaughter room,
The days of our lives numbered yet so anonymous to be conserved.
Before we double the sin and triple its wages,
It is the whistle of hustle amid the shield of love, that we desire;
Not the cries of ghosts on a silver platter.

Oil couldn't mingle with water, but they are both liquids after all;
Every soul will be soon poured out of these racial cocoons.
I beg, as much as I am paralysed ;
If trusting you was a sin, please bless my curse.

Yours truly,
Ukraine.

Linda M. Crate (USA)
Linda is a Pennsylvanian writer. She is the author of 10 poetry chapbooks and four full-length poetry collections. Her works have been published in numerous international magazines and anthologies.
E: veritaserumvial@hotmail.com

LET THIS WAR END

there is still goodness
left in this world,
may sunflowers always
grow;
showing light to those
who need a prayer
of hope—

war is an ugly thing:
maiming, wounding, killing,
ripping families apart;

it does no one any good—

may sunflowers grow,
and peace come swiftly;
let this war end—

how many innocent have already
suffered and died for this
foolishness?
it is never the men who propose
wars that fight,
it is always those who cannot afford
not to fight who always have to;

may the greed of leaders cruel and sharp
pierce them in their own heart.

Mantz Yorke (ENGLAND)
Mantz lives in Manchester. He has published two collections of poetry, and his poems have appeared in a number of print magazines, anthologies and e-magazines in the UK and worldwide.
E: mantzyorke@mantzyorke.plus.com

THE HELSINKI SUMMIT, 2018

In front of flags
they sit together,
a low table
between them.

He on the right
leans towards
the bigger man
who's strangely shrunken.

Cordially,
they shake hands
as if about to begin
a game of chess.

But he on the right
gives his opponent
Morphy's look, knowing
he's already won.

Years to the south,
a country realises
a brutal rain
is set to come.

Lucinda Trew (USA)
Lucinda is an award-winning poet and essayist based in North Carolina. She was named a North Carolina Poetry Society poet laureate (2021 & 2022), and her work is published internationally.
E: lucindatrew@gmail.com

CHEKHOV'S ORCHARD
"Life's all done, just as if I never even lived it ..."
— Anton Chekhov, *The Cherry Orchard.*

it's not quite spring
but coming, titmice
and chickadees float
melisma notes, nubby buds
fleck an aspiring branch
the sun sinks slow, a roseate
stone lingering in sky
and in the east, war

fog of fire and smoke
tanks in shattered city
streets, the sulphur tang
of fury and fear and I wonder
about Chekov's orchard:

will blooms persist or fall
too soon, will flesh of fruit
be sour or sweet, what secret
hides in the stony pit
and will springtime snow
be petal or ash?

Marianne Peel (USA)
Based in Chicago, of Lithuanian, Czech and Slovak heritage, Marianne taught English for 32 years. She has received a number of awards, and her poetry has appeared in magazines and journals worldwide.
E: mariannechina2008@yahoo.com

I REFUSE TO BURY MY HEAD IN THE SAND

I watch the war in Ukraine explode
from a Lazyboy chair blooming with sunflowers.
A woman and her son shelter in a Kyiv subway
burrowing underground to escape the air raids.
She will stay there all night. Her son will fall asleep
with his head cradled in her lap. She will cover
his shivering with her red wool coat.
She will lean against the cinder block wall,
wondering how her 60 year-old father

training sessions for weeks. Her father, a pacifist,
has never held a gun. Such a peaceful man.
She rests her head on the woman's shoulder,
next to her. This woman's husband must also learn
to turn his fingers into a trigger of war.

The President of the Ukrainian Quilter's Association
kindly requests words of support. *We are facing war.
Every warm word is kindly appreciated.* Says she will
translate for the guild members. *We keep praying
for piece*, she writes, spelling *peace* like the scraps
of fabric she births into quilts that keep others warm
at night. Her quilts are flowers blooming in a Ukrainian
field. She longs for spring and all it usually promises
after a dark winter.

A Ukrainian teacher thanks her guardian angel.
Soaked in blood after surviving a Russian missile strike,
her head and face are bandaged. Shards of glass
penetrated her head and face during an airstrike on her apartment.
She vows to do everything for her motherland.

And in Henychesk, near the sea of Azov,
an old woman questions a Russian soldier,
heavily armed. *Who are you?* she asks. The soldier
tells her they have exercises here. *You are occupiers.*

You are enemies. From this moment, you are cursed,
she says. The soldier tells her their discussion
will lead to nowhere. He tells her not to escalate
this situation. Even says *please*. And she offers
sunflower seeds. Tells him to put them in his pockets.
At least sunflowers will grow
on Ukrainian soil
when you die.

Marie C. Lecrivain (USA)

Based in Los Angeles, Marie is a poet, publisher, editor, and ordained priestess. She's the author of several books of poetry and fiction, and her work has been published in a large number of journals worldwide.
E: mariel671@gmail.com
W: www.sybpress.com
W: www.dashboardhorus.blogspot.com
FB: @marieclecrivainauthor

NIHILISTIC EPIPHANY #9

On *PBS*, I watched an old man
tremble with fear as he
lifted a bloodied sheet
atop a gurney
that covered
his son's corpse
then dropped it
and began to weep

I cried with him
for loved ones lost
to other fatal causes
but I've never lost a child
who felt compelled
lay down their life
to defend my country

and his loss will never
get easier to bear
with the loneliness
cruelty and abandonment
war and duty
continue to inflict
on the ones left behind

Anamika Nandy (INDIA)
From Assam, Anamika is an educationist by profession. She loves to pen down whatever comes to her mind, and loves working for the development of society.
E: anamika.sweety1431@gmail.com

SOLDIERS OF GOD

Wake up! Oh, wake up!
You sprightly soldiers of God.
Fervently fluttering its snowy white wings,
The white dove calls.

It comes to awake,
The human caged in Machiavellian frippery.
Prowess that you glow in, through one's Achilles heel,
Is nothing but all transitory.

Time flies! Do not tarry!
Redeem thy souls,
From the clutches of the evil Mephistopheles.

Love is thy sword,
To vanquish all hatred and hegemony.
Empathy thy armour,
To shield against antagonism and disunity.
Equip thy selves with virtues all humanely.
Peace shall then flow like a river,
In all 'We.'

Oh, Sprightly soldiers of God !
Rise and see,
A new dawn of humanity beckons thee!

Marjorie Gowdy (USA)
Marjorie lives in the Blue Ridge mountains. She was Founding Executive Director of the Ohr-O'Keefe Museum of Art in Biloxi, Mississippi. Her poetry has been published worldwide.
E: marjie01@gmail.com
W: www.Blueridgehome.blogspot.com

DYTYNA

Baba brushes baby's fine hair
Crimson ribbons woven into braids

A phone rings, stops short
Clashing cataracts of brick and smoke

Dragon's breath from the east
Flames tossed into young roses

Pyre of satin, biscuits, photos
fire flattens faces fast

Quick tombstones
on blank city streets

Yet the family *Asteraceae*
sows seeds from tailwinds, *nadiya's* fresh soil

Mark Andrew Heathcote (ENGLAND)
Mark is adult learning difficulties support worker based in Manchester.
He is the author of two books of poetry, and has had over 200 poems
published in journals, magazines, and anthologies.
E: mrkheathcote@yahoo.co.uk

EYES WITH CATARACTS

They came as martyrs driving Z-tanks waving red flags.
A convoy of soldiers on military-
exercises to prevent a Ukrainian collapse
to-fix-a disease before it gets pulmonary.
Artillery sent in as a visible persuader
all it says is, surrender-or-we will kill you.
"We're your brother and sisters we're-not-invaders
but once we're here, we're here to stay and take care of you."
They claim that Ukraine is a hornets' nest of fascists
and if they all submit, we might just let you live
but all these red liberating saviour maggots
should get on their bellies and pray to leave their Queen hive.
Their subjugating mother Russia their rogue nation,
shouldn't you pray for your forgiveness that of your neighbour
they-aren't-dogs they don't need or require your affirmations
it's you who are murdering criminal exterminators.
Despots like you always have eyes with cataracts
it's your body and mind that's diseased those-are-the facts.
Let's hope-we-debauch your currency, and you collapse
so we can go on living normally and relax.

Dr. Perwaiz Shaharyar (INDIA)
Perwaiz is a poet, short story writer and critic, and editor at the National Council of Educational Research and Training (NCERT), Ministry of Education. He has published 13 books.
E: drspahmad@gmail.com

WAR AND PEACE

The machines crush human feelings and emotions
The machines make senseless slaves to weaker nations

Weapons are more dangerous to human beings
Because these kill and destroy the whole populations

There have been warmongers in every part of the world
Since the agrarian society and the dawn of civilizations

There are few nations, under the influence of the devils
Which want to make slaves to their neighbouring nations

The war is more devastative than pandemic Covid-19
To protect from it has not been invented any vaccine

Warmongers are like Zombies thirsty for bloods
They are more damaging than quacks and floods

The soldiers become crazy in behaviour during the wars
In dealing with enemies, they don't care about civilians

No one would like war across the whole world
It is imposed by only those who are bullying nations

Wars have left nothing to mankind except blood and tear
For the sake of peace, humanity has always to bear

From the human fraternity of the world, I will appeal
Stop the war, resolve the disputes with a peaceful deal

Mark Saba (USA)
Mark lives in Maine and recently retired as a medical illustrator at Yale University. He has had a number of books published, and his work has appeared widely in literary magazines around the world.
E: msaba@snet.net
W: www.marksabawriter.com
FB: @mark.saba.779

THE DAY THE BOMBS FELL

Men hid in the mountain park
dressed in white, as the white hare,
wolf, and perusing bear looked up
and twigs fell unevenly into snow.

Streams engendered jewels; fountains borne
of Rome lost nothing of their leonine
faces, spouting now for another
two thousand years.

Sun hit hard in the valleys, already suffering
reflections of far-off snow.
Cats perched defiantly in the breeze,
counting their seconds of freedom.

Then the bombs fell, like ripe watermelons
to paint the earth red. Afterwards
the smoke gave up; dark winter clouds
pushed over the ridge, and snow
fell again on the burning towns

while soldiers in the mountainous woods
mistook the sound of thunder
for pealing bells, and saw each other as painted ghosts
too lost among the white winter animals
to know the world below.

Martin Milmo (ENGLAND)
Based in Kent, Martin is a retired EFL teacher, and a member of a local poetry writing group. His enjoys writing poetry and topics for inspiration are aspects of the environment and religious themes.
E: mdpmilmo@hotmail.com

STATIONS OF THE CROSS ... IN UKRAINE

He washes his hands in the flowing of his rhetoric;
I stand becalmed in the white sound of the static.

I point the crosstree of my gun sights
into the eye of the bear's defence of its rights.

The burden he has given is hard to bear;
I fall in a moment of disbelief and despair.

I meet my family, see into my mother's eyes.
We feel each other's terror as we seek solace in our goodbyes

A stander-by sees my distress and supports my exhausted body
With my uniform in blasted rags, bones exposed, bleeding, bloody.

I drag my way through the streets. There are fresh corpses beyond suffering.
I hear a woman with a camera grimace: "Front page in the morning".

A face floats before me, dressed in Russian fatigues;
I fall into the old law of eyes and teeth, hate and intrigues.

Women and children walk past, eyes full of praise and empathy;
I see their new status of refugee and can respond only with pity.

Bleeding slowly out, I hallucinate, and pick up a knife.
I fall again: O, Lord, allow me to take one last life.

It smells of disinfectant, I feel I'm being stripped of my clothes;
I'm being laid out; I sense the start of my death throes.

There's no anaesthetic so they bind me down, hands and feet.
I shudder and fit, scream, a piece of writhing meat.

They calm and settle me, then a surgeon wields his knife;
he looks and sighs "This man's already lost his life".

They wheel him out to his mother, his devoted comrades.

She holds his body, they go back to the barricades.

She wraps him in a shroud, puts him in the soil of his birth;
she gets up from her knees, throws the first handful of earth .

But after three days of darkness, of silenced hatred, of haggling,
Over the broken horizon, a new dawn is seen coming:
a strong blue sky, a bright yellow sun.

My people are fled everywhere
my country in ruins, economies in need of care,
but I am whole again and my independence won.

Martha Fox (USA)
Martha is based in Massachusetts, and has taught young writers throughout her teaching career. She has published a book, a chapbook, and numerous poems in literary journals.
E: marthaffox@comcast.net

AGAIN

Here I am again at my kitchen table
with a noon cup of chicken soup and another newborn
war on TV — this one in Europe, but it's the same black
billow above an airport, the same cross-section ruins
of apartment buildings and charred Renaults
in the Kyiv evening where only a few disbelieving
grandmas are boiling beets for borscht
because everyone fled to the underground
shelter to shudder in stopped, unlighted trains —
babies with dirty diapers, dogs, and retirees —
young ones signing up to fight— and it's
the same silver spoon trembling in my cooling broth,
and nausea, watching footage of families
pack up, stock up, gas up, though it's quiet still,
except for the roosters and the Russian warship
off Zmiinyi Island: *Lay down your arms or
you will be bombed*, Reply: *Russian warship —
go fuck yourself*, from the now dead or captured,
those 13 disappeared Heroes of Ukraine, including
the 23-year-old from Odessa Instagramming
an incoming rocket while I read an incoming
text from my long-time college friend: "I am outside
myself — going crazy" and I think: Oh, Olena, not you,
but a ruthless dictator *again*, another penthouse thug
who sees us through abyss-blue eyes, who knows
what he does and doesn't care (so Father,
do NOT forgive him)
and that is why we, who work so hard to believe
humans lub-dub divinity, are stunned again
by our helplessness — but who am I, Olena, to spit on hope
when in Kharkiv you and your daughter shiver in line
to pick up Kalashnikovs?
So shamed in my snug kitchen, in your name,
and in honour of the unnamed kid from Odessa
who looked up to record the end roaring toward him,
I put down my spoon
and pick up my insignificant pen.

Stephen Poole (ENGLAND)
A retired Metropolitan police officer, Stephen lives in Kent. He has written for a variety of British county and national magazines, and his poetry has been published internationally.
E: typingpoole@yahoo.co.uk

NEVER AGAIN

Not so long ago it was rainbows
and teddies in my window,
now replaced by the blue
and yellow flag of Ukraine.

Futile gestures against overwhelming
waves of death, destruction, and grief.
Thank you, NHS, a similar sentiment as
Never has so much been owed by so many ...

as wet markets continue to trade
and maniacs bomb maternity hospitals,
refugees, like great pools of blood
haemorrhage into neighbouring countries,

the world seemingly unable to stem the flow,
while a tyrant obliterates their homes.
In November, we'll buy our poppies and say:
              Never Again!
       Again, and again, and again ...

Mark Fleisher (USA)

Based in New Mexico, Mark earned a journalism degree and served as a combat news reporter in Vietnam. Published widely, he has recently published his fourth book of poetry.
E: markfleisher111@gmail.com
E: markfleisher333@gmail.com

YOUR STRUGGLE ... OUR STRUGGLE

Nearly a century ago
a tyrant's brutal decrees
starved to death
nearly four million
the Holodomor –
its stark meaning
starvation to inflict death

A decade later
five million including
more than one million
of my people
were murdered by
another horrible hand

Now another tyrant
seeks to erase your
sacred land from
the roster of
democratic nations

You respond with
a collective will
to stand resolute
and resilient,
hoisting the blue
and yellow banner
in resistance to
a ruthless invader

Forces of good
exact a costly price
upon the arrogant aggressor
who crosses lines of decency
killing indiscriminately

The world supports you

for your struggle
is our struggle,
to safeguard
democracy,
uphold humanity,
ensure civility

Slava Ukraini!
Glory to Ukraine!
Glory to the Heroes!

Mary Ellen Fean (REPUBLIC OF IRELAND)
Based in the west of Ireland, Mary has published a collection of poetry, and her work can be seen in magazines and journals across the country.
E: mhodginsfean@yahoo.ie

THE DEPARTED ONES

We bury their bones, anguish
at the loss, but they are not
gone

The dead do not leave us, they
are still here amongst us, I see
them all the time

In a crowded street, I hear their
voices, a familiar turn of phrase
and I am comforted

Perhaps they linger out of love
to ease us gently into the loss, the
loneliness

Of the empty space, a leaf falling
softly, turning slowly as it drops
to earth

Is a loved one is close by, we are
never really alone, the dead are
as near as the living.

Kerfe Roig (USA)
Kerfe is a writer, poet and artist, and resides in New York. Her poetry and art has been featured both online and in several anthologies.
E: memadtwo@gmail.com
W: www.kerferoig.com
W: www.methodtwomadness.wordpress.com

STOP WAR

Stop war. Help.
Where to go?
The life left.

Tried to flee.
Stop war. Help.
For what? What?

So much grief.
Can't go back.
Stop war. Help.

Xanthi Hondrou-Hill (GREECE)
Xanthi is based in Paros and works as a Greek, English and German translator. She also edits the poetry section of an online magazine, and has been published in a large number of magazines and journals.
E: xanthihondrouhill@gmail.com

SEEDS OF PEACE

In ceasefires

I plant at the four corners of the horizon
where the blood of my brothers
blackens in the sun
seeds of peace.

In the ceasefires

I light candles
to light the paths of the spirit
traced and lived by Gandhi.

In the ceasefires I open
the door to strangers
to come and share
bread, water, roses.
In the ceasefires I build
with my hands
the dreams of children
of the whole world.

In the ceasefires I touch
the hearts of those around me
to erase the pain of the past,
to join together to become a circle
To become dance, joy, song.

In the ceasefires I plant
The seeds of my lyrics
To speak in the tongues of the world
to become an eternal hymn for peace.

Todd Matson (USA)
Todd is a Licensed Marriage and Family Therapist practising in North Carolina. His poems have been published in a number of health care and counselling publications.
E: tmatson4@hotmail.com

ANACHRONISMS AND ANGELS

What is an ageing,
maniacal, power hungry,
bloodthirsty Russian tyrant
with no retirement plan to do?

Relinquish power
and the protection of
the regime and oligarchs?

People held hostage
by tyrants – exploited
and impoverished, ruled
and oppressed, lied to, poisoned
and pushed out of 6th story windows
are not especially fond of their retired
dictators who've spent a lifetime picking
their pockets and murdering their loved ones.

With no retirement plan,
what is an ageing tyrant to do?

Go retro?
Become an
imperial tzar
as in days of old?

Rebuild a long-lost empire
by bombing innocent men, women and
children of neighbouring countries into submission?

Lay waste residential buildings
and civilian infrastructure with cluster munitions,
vacuum bombs, precision short-range missiles and cruise missiles?

Leave civilians wounded and dying
with no shelter, food, heat, power or water?
Create millions of refugees, widows and orphans?

Murder millions of refugees, widows and orphans
by relentlessly bombing refugee evacuation corridors?

Commit war crimes and
become an international pariah?
Hope against hope
that in the age of the internet
truth will not penetrate a newly constructed
iron curtain of lies told to keep loyal subjects captive?

Enough about Vladimir Putin.

What are people facing an
existential threat of genocide,
annihilation and captivity to do?

Ask the people of Ukraine.

Ukrainian civilians
join Ukrainian troops,
women join men, young
join old to fight on the side
of the angels, to fight for the right
to life, liberty and the pursuit of happiness.

They take no prisoners.
To the young Russian conscripts
duped into murdering innocents under
the guise of being deployed for harmless military
drills, they give phones, have them to call their mothers
to come get them and take them home. Come, take them home.

Soo Strong (ENGLAND)
Soo lives in Norfolk, and co-leads a local monthly writing group. She has written poetry for years, but has only just started sharing it, and will be shortly be publishing a collection of her work.
E: mindfullifeeast@gmail.com
FB: @soostrongcoachingcourses
W: www.mindfullifeeast.thinkific.com

THE HEARTBREAK OF WAR

Skin and bones so activated,
As their independence is decimated.
Heart and mind just cannot settle,
This escalating pressure kettle.

The scale of this, all so unjust,
Halting it becomes a must.
People fleeing for some safety,
Scared and anxious, all so hasty.

One day tucked up in their bed
Next Putin's lost his head!
Caught in chaos all around,
Peace solutions not yet found.

Can't they see we're interconnected,
The whole damn world we are affected.
Families, goods and different cultures,
Torn apart by histories vultures.

Our hearts go out to all in Ukraine,
Let's find solutions, let peace reign.
Respect to all those Russians resisting,
Despite their leader's cruelty persisting.

We're all a part of common humanity,
Take greatest care, protect your sanity.
Hold a hand upon your heart,
In times like these this is an art.

Tandra Mishra (INDIA)
Tandra is a writer and poet, with a post graduation in English Literature. Her poems have been published in magazines and journals worldwide, and her first book of poetry has just been published.
E: tandramishra2019@gmail.com
FB: @tandra.mishra.58

THROW ALL THE BAYONETS INTO THE OCEAN

Throw all the missiles, all the bayonets into the ocean,
Not on the houses, children, men and women.
Bury them inside the deep water, let them rust,
So that they never come back and dare human body touch.

The Ocean is deep, wide and blue.
Large enough to hold all the sins you do.

Don't make fool others and not show your foolishness.
God has not given bombs or bayonets in your palms.
God has given brain, heart and kindness.
Use them and make a peaceful universe.

The earth is bestowed with herbs and gems.
Use your brain to use them for humans.
Throw your greed, your lust into the ocean.
To stop one more war, to stop destruction.

Throw your anger, your despise, hatred into the ocean.
Read science, read astronomy, read the physics with concentration.
The universe has been created with a long journey.
And not in a single day, from the comb comes the honey.

Don't spoil God's creation, His mission,
To live happily with each other using His donation.
If you wish to rule over a country,over a nation.
Make sure first you are not going to stab God's heart, His emotion.

Stephen Ferrett (SCOTLAND)
Since an early age, Stephen has always had a passion for writing and poetry, and has recently published his first children's book, with a sequel on its way.
E: stephen.ferrett@mottmac.com

DAUGHTERS OF UKRAINE

The women you are, and the women that you will become, defines everything that is pure, loving, free and so right in this world
Your pain, and that of your people, wracked by oppression, suppression, aggression, and greed, is everything that is wrong in this world
My admiration for you, knows no bounds, you are the spirit and embodiment of your homeland.
A land of precious souls that will not bow down, will fight for everything that they hold dear. Willing and ready to make the ultimate sacrifice for your precious Tryzub.
Every Man, every Woman, every Son, and every Daughter of Ukraine, we standby you, salute you and reach out to you.
Calm blue skies and joyful golden wheat fields will abound. Radiating the vibrance of you and your nation, as we are entwined in the colours of your flag
You are the Daughters of Ukraine, we are stood by your side in our thoughts, in our hearts and in our souls.

Sara Sarna (USA)
Recently retired from the field of health care and living in Wisconsin, Sara is now a poet and actor. She has published widely, and her work has been heard on stage and radio.
E: sarna1991@hotmail.com

SOLDIERS

He stands in the lane,
you in the rubble,
rage your only weapon, words
that lie in wait on your tongue.

But you see his face,
forlorn, like yours.
His hands by his sides,
ten fingers, like yours.
Dark smudges under his eyes,
purple shadows, like yours.

He imagines himself
far from here
in his mother's kitchen,
washing the berries
she will put in a pie,
sunlight on
the pink of her cheeks,

but he is here,
watching you imagine
you bask in the blue
of dining room walls,
sit at the table with your father
as children race
up the gravel path,
sticky with juice of apple,
and pear and joy,

but you are here,
searching for memories
in bits of your attic
now scattered on cobblestones.
You and the soldier,

both longing for home.

Dr. Sarah Clarke (ENGLAND)

Now based near London, Sarah lived in the Middle East for 15 years where she ran a non-profit program using pet dogs to enhance the life and social skills of children with communication difficulties.
E: sarah@dscwll.com
FB: @Baloosbuddies
FB: @sarahclarke888

STRENGTH

She nods wisely
To the left
To the right
Always carefully balanced
Centred
Turning her head towards the sun
As it traverses the sky on a predictable path
This she has done for as long as she can remember
Always catching the last rays
Before the sun lays down for the night

As she bows
She knows tomorrow may be her last
Shattered not by natural elements
But by madness
Tonight she stands strong
Her roots planted firmly in her homeland
Steadfast in her determination
To show off her yellow ruffed bonnet with pride
Until the last possible moment
She will not be broken
Not ever.

Dr. Sajid Hussain (PAKISTAN)
Sajid is a Master Trainer, senior teacher of Chemistry, and a former school Principal. He has written more than 700 poem, and is published in several international anthologies and magazines.
E: teacherimsb@gmail.com

A WEARY SIGH

Mist of moan spreads in invaded land,
Savage act in sovereignty of a nation,
Dress the clothes of bloodshed to innocent,
Trumpets blow in war on the limbs of an infant,
Blasted waves of bursting clouds are all around,
In loudness terrify immersed souls,
Thrown into at random bumped their pieces,
The dead shocked pawns get no more breaths,
A death shadow on a fair sunlit landscape,
Prevails on helpless victims in tragic moments,
The depths of sorrows on absorbed dread the faces,
The thick fog of despair hangs on a unresting,
Frightened a child in the darkness of bombardment,
Tries to seek a fragile spider's web as a shelter,
No soft-thoughts of budding love he has,
Gone astray dropping soul of his sweet dreams,
Touches the above waves of a tempest of fear,
Lost in hopeless vision of frowned uncertainty,
choked by the thorns of severe adversity,
The petals of a rose are being crushed by stones,
Collapses are being coloured like a fairy tale,
Constant glided shelling for fear held terror,
Killing as arbitrary as cyclones of opposing winds,
Destroy everything what come across to them.
Still the smoke of blasting flashes steady flames.

Sandy Phillips (ENGLAND)
Sandy lives in London and enjoys writing poetry, flash fiction, and articles for psychic magazines. She has also had a book published.
E: Sandy.phillips72@yahoo.co.uk

THE PEOPLE'S WAR

As daylight dimmed into night,
the bombardment began,
A baptism into war for the innocents
Dipped in dismay, every woman and man.

A barrage of noise breaks up the land
Hour after long terrifying hour,
Fear galloped up gullets and down in dirt,
Tongues thick, yellow and sour.

They wept at the carnage collapsed around,
What sacrifices hung in red shreds
On the altar of unsought war,
Given as a blessing bestowed on all their heads.

A few were sent ahead to scout about,
A hidden sniper's bullet seared the air,
A body dropped, stirring up dust from charred rags
Into the sun's early morning glare.

Mars hung raw in the strangely quiet dawn,
Out of the haze a bird's solo song
Seemed out of place; Dante's Inferno over
Fireworks of the nigh now gone.

Day is filled with troops on the move with
Ammunition and orders to be read.
Among the debris boots and limbs of
Soldiers and child alike; all of them dead.

S. D. Kilmer (USA)
S. D. resides in Central New York State and is a retired Counsellor and Family Conflict Mediator. He has been published in multiple international anthologies and literary e-zines.
E: sdkilmerllc@gmail.com
W: www.SDKilmer.com

DESPERATE ROAD TO FREEDOM

It's snowing. They're storming.
Brothers from the East are shelling,
The Borderlands, the Ukraine.
Motherland's destruction and pain.
Buildings and homes and farms.
Force a peaceful people to arms.
Ukraine is not yet dead.
Their mothers and daughters journey ahead
The desperate road for safety and bread.
While Fathers and sons spare neither soul nor body, hastily
to regain national freedom.
As the dew does in the sunshine,
Their enemies will perish;
God will still smile and cherish
the Borderlands people
Glory and freedom will remain with them unchanged,
The Children of Ukraine.

Rohan Facey (JAMAICA)
Rohan is a high-school teacher and a multiple-award winning contemporary poet, songwriter and playwright. He has contributed to both local newspapers and international anthologies.
E: PoeticFirerf@yahoo.com

UNDER SIEGE

The bullets whistled again, beloved.
Not as referees – but as emissaries
of doom and gloom; shattering the chords
of peace to useless slivers.

This morning,
the sun did not open her eyes-
for the Dark Man walked here
with a blueprint - fashioned in hell.

And the bell kept tolling –
again and again in haunting succession ...
"In the sweet by and by" burdens
our lent hours, anxious
voices whisper the inevitable: "Who's next?"

The bullets whistled again, beloved.
fatal, fractured notes
like a musician losing a melody.

The guns march around our existence –
Leering like minions from hell.

And the Dark Man laughs – for the gallows
have no power.

Russell Willis (USA)
Russell lives in Vermont. He has been published in over 25 online and print journals and 16 anthologies.
E: willisdrr63@gmail.com
W: www.REWillisWrites.com

THE PATH: A BOMBED-OUT BRIDGE IN IRPIN

Wandering through or past
The ones who flee the bombs
Across a makeshift bridge of
Pieces of their normal lives
Planks and girders overflowed
Ignoring fear and broken hearts
Until safer on the other side
But not yet safe upon their path

Takes grace to tread the path
That wanders through or past
Another's soul or mind or heart
With no thought of self or right
No damage of the collateral sort
No insistence that this path alone
Leads to the pot of gold deserved
The merit of who holds the keys
Wandering through or past
The ones we keenly disregard
The ones that don't deserve
Or even know that sort of grace
Ignoring soul or mind or heart
And thus disfiguring our own
The cost of that collateral sort
Insisting this the only path
There are no keys to unlock grace
No currency, not even gold
No weapon that ensures the
Perseverance of our goals
But grace alone, that which is love
That which is peace that conquers fear
That which is solace to our ears
Whispered as a lullaby
The whispered lullaby
That drowns the bully's boast
The space to catch a breath
Comforts like a warm embrace
The differences that complement

That unify, that coalesce
The grace to tread the path
The one that wanders through or past

Rupsingh Bhandari (NEPAL)
Based in the Karnali province, Rupsingh is a writer, poet and social activist. He has published poems, articles, and short stories in several international journals, magazines and online platforms.
E: dirupss44@gmail.com

LET US REQUEST DNIEPER

The river Dnieper
Which slithers out from Valdai Russia to Ukraine
Is sleepless without knowing any reasons
As the old grandma,
Dnieper never confuse by the conspiracy of the world
Now swelling with many unanswered questions
Without any words ...

The birds of Eurasia:
    Waterfowl,
    Waders,
    Skuas,
    Auks,
    Gulls,
    Passerines,

Never change their song wherever they fly across those land
Are mourn— voiceless,
They never mimic other's lyrics

Now, are frightened with strange smell of gunpowder— the evil song
Watching the bombs with fire-tails flying over the sky
Trembling on the potholes of uncertainty
Chewing their innocence ... clueless

The fearless wild animals:
    Eurasian elk
    Marten,
    Mouflon,
    Roe deer,
    Wildcat,
    Wild pig,
    Wolf

are puzzled by the tanks which are throwing up the deaths
Walking as the snake's lateral undulation ...
Throbbing between the hollowness of wilderness
And the firecrackers over the sky ... hunching their heads—hopelessly

Now, let us stop our never ending arguments
Let them ask:
The solutions of the war,
Let them hum their common song
Let us ask them to pair off for group performance
Now, let us stop languages of war
And listen to their unchanged song, their unspoiled dance
Let us request the Dnieper to dissolve
Their misunderstanding and egos
Into the Black Sea,
Silently!

Rohini Sunderam (CANADA / INDIA / BAHRAIN)
Rohini is a semi-retired advertising copywriter. She ran the Bahrain Writers' Circle for ten years. Her poems have appeared worldwide and she has had a number of collections of poetry published.
E: rohinisunderam@hotmail.com
Twitter: @corpoetry

THE SUNFLOWER AND THE SKY

What can the sunflower say to the sky?
It follows the sun; it never asks why.
The rockets fly past, the tanks they roll on
Winter sets in with a cold that is long.
Sanctions are threatened, their impact is hollow
Who thinks of the people; who knows their sorrows?

What can the sunflower say to the sky?
It follows the sun; it never asks why.
De-communization, the anthem they sang
While the clappers on church bells solemnly rang
Kyiv, Kharkiv, Odessa and Donbas
They cringed and they cowered with every blast.

What can the sunflower say to the sky?
It follows the sun; it never asks why.
Armoured vehicles push into Ukraine
Who thinks of the people; who knows their pain?
Every border's attacked, the world wrings its hands
But they still do not move, nor yet make a stand.

What can the sunflower say to the sky?
It follows the sun; it never asks why.
It's your land, your country, you're ready to fight
No matter the foe, no matter its might.
To the last inch, the last breath, last woman, or man.
Though the world does nothing, the World understands.

What can the sunflower say to the sky?
It follows the sun; it cannot ask why.

Roy J. Adams (CANADA)
A retired professor, Roy published his first poem at the age of 75. Now at 81, he has published a chapbook, a full collection, and poetry in journal and anthologies worldwide.
E: adamsr@mcmaster.ca

QUANDRY

After lurking for weeks
He strikes
Indiscriminately
Wounding, killing
Women, children,
The sick, the lame
And still you stand

He threatens:
Poison, famine, pestilence,
Immolation
And still you stand

We, your friends provide
Refuge, materiel, refusal of
Sustenance that saps
His strength
But not enough
To make him stop
And still you stand

If you ceased struggling
He might let you live
Some of you
But then you would be
Forever his
To command

We honour your mettle
Would like to do more:
Planes, tanks, missiles,
Boots galore
Enough to prevail or
The end of you?
The end of us?
The end of him?
The end of days?

And what of
The more cautious
Course
Will it gain us
Gain you
The ends we seek or
Nothing at all?

Rita B. Rose (USA)
Based in New York, Rita is a published author, poet and playwright, and Long Island's LGBTQ poet laureate. Her poems have appeared in various anthologies, both abroad and in the USA.
E: stonewallrusty@aol.com

SELF- PORTRAIT OF ALEXEY
"Sight is the noblest sense of man." - Albrecht Dürer

I was looking in the mirror adjusting the hoodie over
my knit hat when sirens wailed and church bells pealed
            there was hardly time to take cover
    I coiled in my tub   hands over head
reciting prayers as glass shattered and walls toppled around me
    I heard incessant groans
then a long scream   the building shivered and swayed
    it was then I realized   the squeals   were steel girders
genuflecting under Russian missiles   striking   my apartment building
    How did I make it out alive? I drew in an acrid whiff   waded
through the rubble   I groped along dark scorched walls
a stark sliver of lit window   guided me   moved me forward
alongside its gaping hole   was a hurled remnant of a reproduction
a self-portrait of an artist I purchased in Ocean Plaza, Kyiv
it peered through the fallout   our eyes set upon each other
his slashed sleeves were worse for wear   seemed he too were battling
for Ukrainian freedom   still   his fur jacket seemed inviting
enough to nuzzle in   I carried his cadre as if a long-lost friend
    Voices in the street shouted hey you need a rope as television cameras
panned the damage   a photographer snapped my trepidation
        framed were my broken dreams   I searched sweltering clouds
        dipped my beard into the cool ochre of a fragmented sun
hand resting on the heart of my torn jacket   my other hand clung
to the stoic painting of Dürer as the world witnessed war in real time
        and did nothing—in death-like stillness
                              we turned away.

Richard Spisak (USA)
Richard lives in Tennessee. He is a professional video editor, producer, and an award-winning poet. He has recently published a 300 plus page volume of collected poetry.
E: rwspisak@vivaldi.net
W: www.NewMercuryMedia.com/pnn.html
FB: @rwspisak
Twitter: @rwspisak

DO NOT RAIN BULLETS ON UKRAINE

Do not rain bullets in Ukraine.
Don't play chicken with my world
As you pack your brighty flighty banners bolden
there in stolen gold, I swear! So noted.
UNCOUNTED.
Accounted , Miscounted Dismounted.
Discounted villagers despoiled,
like some useless rack of neatly stacked.
Unnumbered Boys and girls unpacked.

Sure, you'll knock a few walls down
spread some pointless furtive fugitive blood around
Your thrusting Guts
Give grave LUSTY brave vict'ry
to UNSAVOR A EMFEEBLED FAMISHED few.

Annual
Blow away a thou' or two.
Careless Craft though there's PLENTY bullets left A RAFT
you'd laugh! Resenty! Presently!
As the sleepy blooded lines
go fore and aft
Uttered muttered
ANY LESS WOULD BE A LAUGH!

Minefields planted promise flowery death,
an innocent murderers childlike theft.

How about this slighter silvered few
a brand new brass hued
bullets true
we've scarce a millions left.
Unused YOU KNOW's a kind of theft!

Don't cha like the noisome rattle

as we stir up all the blinkered cattle.
Soon it will be quite inevitable
As we drive the stanking clanging TANK
right through the freshly RED CARPETED vestibule
OVER THE DEAD you once knew.

Yeah wheel Drive over a couple bodies
Sure and TRUE we know
it makes us naughty
But here beneath my waving flag so haughty
as I on this rotted corpses curse take a drag and make ,
I'll take my coffee mixed with flag!
Sure it might cost, some bleeding horror
honour bound to sag.
If I'd tasted death without a Coroner
a millions left to squander slaughter theft
and more.

Would I these brighty bullets waste
though fonder
Just to save the neighbours daughter?

Rhonda Parsons (USA)
Based in Illinois, Rhonda performed poetry at the first Prelude to Art Scene in Spring of 2021. She has released one book of poetry, and is currently working on a second.
E: lilyspanda7@yahoo.com

SERRIED LINES

We stand in serried lines
wearing the armour of love

We stand in serried lines
hearts united across the globe

We stand
we stand
we stand
in serried lines
with the people
the animals of Ukraine

We stand for justice
we stand for peace

We stand to end oppression
violence
and secular greed

We stand in serried lines
battling for the Promised Dawn
with swords of Truth and certitude
and shields of steadfastness
we shall be victors

We stand in serried lines
for always it shall be.

Wilda Morris (USA)
Wilda lives in Illinois. She is a former president of the Illinois State Poetry Society, and a widely-published poet who has won awards for her free and formal verse and haiku.
E: wem@ameritech.net
W: www.wildamorris.blogspot.com

SHRAPNEL
Beginning with a line by Alice Major ...

wind sharp as shrapnel
blows through the mass of refugees
trudging westward
hoping to get out of reach
of Russian bombs and missiles
backpacks weigh them down
though they have brought so little
from abandoned or burned-out homes
small feet tire
as do those of grandparents
labouring along with canes or walkers
struggling to keep up
sharper than the wind
is the anger and despair
from doubts they can ever return
to Mariupol, City of Mary
the city of their birth
the burial place of ancestors
the home where they raised children
fear they will never again
attend the music festival
and the festival of contemporary arts
or stroll through the City Garden
or take their children to the zoo
and the parks they loved
never worship in the church
where they were baptized and married
or the mosque where they prayed
but even sharper, grief
for the child
the brother
sister
neighbour
dead beneath the ruins
in the city that is now called a cemetery

Abigail George (SOUTH AFRICA)
Abigail is an essayist, blogger, poet, playwright, and short story writer. She has written 12 books (including two novels), and her work has appeared all over Africa.
E: abigailgeorge79@gmail.com
FB: @abigailgeorgewriter

THE RUSSIAN INVASION OF UKRAINE

Into the window of despair that is written all over your face. What do you know of terror? Walk towards me is all I asked. You could not love or rather could not love me. I must forgive myself for stepping into the nonchalant river. Two vessels of light. You were a body of water and I floated on my back looking at pictures of classmates from high school that had no memory of me. You would explode into view on those afternoons and now I have the sun but that is all I have. The sun is a coin and I am a turning point. Choose me. Choose not to love me. Grant me wisdom. Give me insight into the wedlock of relationships. So, I take this coin and place it into the slot machine with hope. All I receive is grief. I go back to writing my poetry. I go back to scrawling. You're not here. You're not here. You're not here and then I am unhappy. For a brief time, you kept me going like a ticking clock. You kept me alive. A woman's primary function is to think like a woman and find peace in the world and partake of it and then to find a man of her own and give that peace to him. Not just to be taken up by the man but to understand that as far as slot machines go there will always be hope. There is far too much war and conflict in the world. In my veins, rushing through air, in the marginalised throat of a bird, at a cellular level. It is winter here now. I close my eyes and feel a cataclysm. Your breath, your eyes and I open my eyes and see a forest of trees gaining on me. The branches reach out to me and the moment is divine. I should drink to forget you. I should smoke but I don't. You're not here. I imagine your ghost. Terror in my blood an eclipse. I hold the sun and it is like a volcano. You are now on top of a mountain, and I am into the ice river where I can never be found again.

Rose Menyon Heflin (USA)
Rose is an award-winning writer and artist living in Wisconsin. She had published a number of books, and her poetry has appeared in journals and anthologies spanning four continents.
E: rosemenyonheflin@gmail.com

REFUGEE MEMORIES: A TANKA SEQUENCE

I.
Precious memories
Drawn upon in times of need
Of those bygone days
Days of tight togetherness
Days of happiness and peace

II.
Days of calm beauty
Days of small, mundane pleasures
Days of great laughter
Days of friends and families -
All those days before the war

III.
Before the fighting
Before conscription happened
Before the bombs dropped
Before all the suffering
Before you fled for your life

IV.
When you had great dreams
When you had a full belly
When you had purpose
When you had a loving home
When you had a bright future

V.
Now all that is gone
As air raid sirens echo
And you find yourself
In a nebulous limbo
With just memories

Agnieszka Filipek (REPUBLIC OF IRELAND / POLAND)
Polish-born Agnieszka's work has appeared in over 60 publications internationally, and has been translated into a number of languages.
E: agnifilipek@yahoo.ie
FB: @polmnieapoltobie

POPPIES

the sky cracks
rivers flow with blood

soldiers flood the earth
singing the lullaby

their weapons shining
like jewellery

and under their feet
anonymous bones

First published in *The Stony Thursday Book*, Ireland.

Agnieszka Wiktorowska-Chmielewska (POLAND)
Based in Krakow, Agnieszka is a poet, writer, playwright, animator, editor and scriptwriter. She is the author of eight poetry books, as well as numerous radio plays, dramas and songs for children.
E: agnieszkawch@poczta.onet.pl
FB: @agnieszka.wiktorowskachmielewska

SKETCHING

The herons at the backwaters,
while in the shelters
they try to replace the anxiety
with a few minutes of sleep
in the sleeping bags from Decathlon.
my dear friends, grey-feathered,
fly over the city on fire and spread the (s)peace.
so it finally quietens
the brassy question
Почему?/Чому?

Amit Parmessur (MAURITIUS)
Amit is a private tutor based in Quatre-Bornes. His poems have appeared in over 165 magazines, journals and anthologies worldwide.
E: ameet_p23@yahoo.co.uk

HEROES

teem in this land where the blue sky used to
sit on fields of flowers, yellow, peaceful—
where a grandfather, doing it for his
grandchildren, gets into a fistfight with
a soldier carrying a huge rifle.
Where mothers, during mortal air raids, are
giving birth in shelters, metro stations;
where my friend is practising how to shoot

to defend her shy self, and her neighbours.
In this land scarred by scary disasters,
fatherless children sleep with their pets and
a smile in bomb shelters they never knew.
An old woman confronts an enemy,
offers him sunflower seeds, telling him,
"Take these. Put them in your pockets, so at
least sunflowers will grow when you die here."

A man with Down Syndrome, wishing this gloom
to be noonday, bakes bread for his soldiers.
In this land where the blue sky used to sit
on yellow flowers, we find keen teachers
doing classes in bunkers and basements.
We find funny farmers towing away
enemy tanks with their tractors. We find
nurses and doctors caring for merry

babies while bombs are dropping, shots are fired,
sirens blaring. What is happening in
this country is happening somewhere else—
every day. They are everywhere—heroes,
heroes who love sunlight in a blue sky.

Amrita Valan (INDIA)
Amrita is from Bangalore. Her debut collection of 50 poems, and her collection of 17 short stories, have both recently been published.
E: amritavalan@gmail.com

THE FAIRY LORE

In my childhood a big white
Matte book
Gold scrolling across the front
Cover
Fascinated me.

Ukrainian Fairy Tales
A symbol
Of pleasure and magic
Of an age

Now remote.

Now gun battles rule
Mercenaries overrun the capital
Looters on the prowl.

Tanks like grim tankas
Offer gunmetal propriety,
Close in across the border

Love thy neighbour
Do not covet his possessions

Seems like a fairy tale adage
Today.

Lovely Mother Russia
Your tales of Gorky and Gogol
Sholokov and Pasternek
Enchanted too
And you were the mother
Of folklore and fairy tales
Where the fair and just
Won always.

Today's television rips the
Enchantment off the screen

The myopic leaders goose-stepping,
In vain glory of follies.

The art and culture
Of war torn lands
Join hands
Hanging heads in shame.

Anna Dunlap (USA)
Anna lives in Colorado, and was a rehabilitation counsellor for developmentally disabled adults. Now retired, she is focusing on her writing, and has recently been published in two anthologies.
E: amdunlap1@msn.com

ST. GEORGE THE GREEK MAY BE ROLLING OVER IN HIS GRAVE IN ISRAEL

'Z' is the Russian meme of the moment, splashed
across billboards in orange & black stripes
symbol of the ribbon of St. George
highest honour given for glory in battle.

It is said the colours mean fire & gunpowder
or death & resurrection of St. George
or black two-headed eagles on yellow
escutcheons used by Imperial soldiers.

It is said St. George joined the Roman army
& died untimely, 303 anno domini. He may
have been decapitated for Christianity, or he
may have decapitated a dragon for Christianity

or his acts may be known to God only.
It is said the saint is promiscuous, patron
of warriors & farmers, shepherds & lepers
peacekeeping missions, entire cities & countries.

It is said, with St. George's blessing
Z is for Za pobedu! For victory! Or zveri, beast
or Z is for zlo, evil; for homage to invasion
for nukes against molotovs made by babushkas.

Bill Cushing (USA)
Recently retired after 23 years of teaching in California, Bill was named as one of the Top Ten Poets of L.A, and has been published in a large number of literary journals, magazines, and newspapers.
E: piscespoet@yahoo.com

HAKA
(written March 2022 to honour Ukraine)

Defeat birthed these primal tribesmen;
harsh turmoil raised them, so they began
celebrating life with clenched fists that
hammer chests, then open to slap forearms.
Blue scars from youth form patterns,
swirls and spirals grow from spacious faces enlarged
by eyes that bulge, by cheeks that widen,
by tongues that snake over jutting jaws.

The air shimmers from muscular vibrations.
They leap and stamp side to side,
slap the ground in defiant rage, a sharp
dance that displays fury for at least
one more day. The warriors offer unbroken stares,
challenge anyone who dares engage:
"Take my head. Gnaw on my bones, suck the marrow,
but never doubt what ferocity we will return to you."

Ndue Ukaj (KOSOVO)
Ndue is a writer, essayist, and literary critic, and has won several awards for his work. He has published four poetry books, one short story collection, and two literary criticism books.
E: ndue.ukaj@gmail.com

INFERNO IS ON EARTH
(Night dialogue with Dante Alighieri)
Translated by Edita Kuçi Ukaj

In middle age - even if you remain on inferno
you have handful of nostalgia, some wrinkled memories
that crawls like your weary feet.
But the children of war have their memories on toys,
to the last pages of books full of adventures.
When they open the window, they see smoke,
smoke, and sadness. This new chapter of their life is being written
through the rubble and the roar of arms.

Dante – inferno is on earth each time there is no freedom
and the cold power of weapons extends over human destinies.

It's March, the beautiful season.
Winter is in its last throes.
But there is no open sky in Ukraine.

The smoke of war has darkened the horizons
and the earth is covered with fear.

A child in the Kyiv hospital expects to disappear to a new place
which is called Security.
This place on earth seems not to exist today, Dante.
There is the poison of hate and sorrow on earth.
There is darkness and the veins of hatred want to burst.

It is darkness and soul darkness are more horrific than that of hell.

Everything is written and said:
War is terrible.

"No – he cannot do that,"- said the sick girl's mother
and closed her eyes to see a little light,
but there are ruins ahead her,
where the dreams of the innocent are dissolved.

The girl cries. Is in pain. Oxygen in the hospital is at risk of spending

Food is limited. Only news
and political statements are abundant.
No one know the pain of a child leaving nightclothes,
bags of toys, and disappear away. Escape is ice-cold as death.

And war is a harsh continent where the unfortunate beings dwell
them that forget their names, tear down dreams
and turn into fear.

Dante, how to get together children's tears -
and with it to create a great river
where all sinners can enter and bathe in it.

Dante, today I cried with the voice of the little girl in a hospital in our earth.
She takes cure to heal her sickness
while hearing the alerts of war and said: I want to escape.
Her cries have entered my room, like the spear.
She needs one who leads her out of the inferno.
You know how it goes,
Therefore, you ought to appear
and bring humans out of the fiery hell of suffering.

Dante, you know that one day the weapons will cease,
shameless leaders, will sit at tables
and will sign a peace document which they tear up whenever they want.
But their madness pays from innocent and the generations to come.

Therefore, we need to make the earth better,
to decrease the amount of fear
and increase the amount of goodness.
Then undo the word war
and with it, to burn all cursed borders
and in their place to plant magnificent flowers and trees.

Bryan Franco (USA)
Bryan is a gay, Jewish poet from Maine. He has performed on stage and in Zoom open mics, and his work has been published in a large number of international magazines and journals.
E: francobryani@gmail.com

A MOST UNUSUAL WAY TO PROPAGATE HOPE

Years ago, I planted sunflowers
in my front yard from seed.
The seed package showed
white, yellow, orange, red,
maroon, purple, pink and peach flowers.

They were different heights and diameters.
I planted them along the walkway
from the driveway to the front steps.
They looked like stringbean-skinny scarecrows with
green overalls and different coloured sunhats.
They grew and bloomed and produced new buds
as they also withered and shed petals.

There is beauty in watching a flower
hang on for dear life as it
gets nibbled by bugs and ages.
Eventually they drop seeds,
but it's healthier for new buds
to cut off old flowers before
their offspring bloom.

Sunflowers are not perennial where I'm from,
but every plant is perennial somewhere.
I'm not sure if they grow back on their own in Ukraine,
but Ukrainians who chose to stay and fight
as bombs turn towns into ashes and ruins
offer invading soldiers sunflower seeds
so this symbol of hope and life can grow
from composted bodies of those who destroyed
their homeland to grow new hope.

Or

the Ukrainians who give sunflower seeds
to Russian soldiers
just
hope

the soldiers will eat the seeds,
become conscientious objectors,
and go home.

Brian Wake (ENGLAND)
Brian was born and currently lives in Liverpool. He has been writing poetry for over forty years, and has had eight books of poems published. He has also had his work published internationally.
E: brianwake1@btinternet.com

TO WHAT SHALL THEY RETURN

To what shall they return those patriotic boys,
Those girls with children wailing in their arms?
What devastated land awaits where smoke has spiralled
Into doom grey cloud and blocks of homes are absences
And ash to fuse with bodies stiffened in the carcasses of cars?
To what shall they return with nothing to unpack, when
All commotion ends, except accounts of incidents.

From where shall weeping mothers yet emerge intact
To rake the embers for their loved ones' furnaced frames
From darkness into more on what were once ploughed
Fields and avenues. And what can be reborn in nuclear soil?
What smouldering branches shall await the blackened snow
Or snow survive the blistering earth? And who shall say
How desperately they fought in order not to fail or fall,
Those patriotic boys, those girls with children wailing
In their arms, into the horror of eternity?

Carol Tahir (USA)
Carol lives in Southern California. She was a licensed Cosmetologist for 48 years. When she retired she wanted a new hobby, so turned to poetry.
E: akittykay_66yahoo.com

WEEPING LAND

Puppeteers work the strings
Humans beat the drums of greed
Aluminium titanium birds fill the sky
dropping terror and destruction on a crying land.
Ankylosarus stampede, churning the ground
leaving mayhem like a ship's wake.
And the Puppeteers laugh and laugh
as they collect their wages of human life and suffering.

The clouds wring out cleansing water on a dirty world.
Cherry red oxygen bound iron lies in rutted puddles,
left to dry in a sodden land,
It feeds the roots of forgotten dreams
A place of blooms where once destruction reigned
The sun returns, the hopes grow
Maybe not in places you know
The soil doesn't forget but people do.

Chua Rui Heng (SINGAPORE)
Chua is a 16 year-old student, and has only recently started to develop an interest in poetry after being given an assignment to write a poem by his teacher.
E: ruiheng06@gmail.com
Instagram: @chua_rh

CONFLICT, FROM THE EYES OF AN UKRAINIAN

an orange blanket covers the walls
turning this once lifeless district alive
consuming my memories and childhood
spitting out ash and soot in return.

lifeless husks littered the streets.
fabric flapping along with the chilling wind.
cobblestone streets stained a beautiful crimson red
bringing colour to this drab district.

an infestation of silver flies has broken out,
with every new one announcing their arrival with a bang.
strong enough to pierce through us,
leaving the city a shell of its former self.

i couldn't help but cry,
as i bid farewell
to what used to be
and what remained of
my home.

Don Beukes (SOUTH AFRICA / ENGLAND)
Don taught English and Geography in both South Africa and the UK. He has been anthologized in numerous collections, and his work translated into a number of languages.
E: donbeuks2@gmail.com

SYMPHONY FOR KYIV

Siren Lullaby – It began as a faint distant growl like a
den of lions advancing to its prey – Steadily, stealthily.
The air static with fiery collective tension, even the birds
missed their morning song. Warnings were shared but we
never dared to thinking the worst in this proud country of ours
where golden eagles kiss golden sacred domes rising to the
heavens, casting a protecting cautionary eye over us.
The peace suddenly shattered by invading missiles
puncturing denting flattening fracturing maiming
shaming claiming destroying deleting erasing.

Alien Sounds – Apocalyptic rumblings deafen
our ears scarring our minds causing mayhem
of all kinds. Where to hide who to grab what
to salvage who to follow which way who to
trust so many cars unavoidable scars a
broken bridge humanity flees glass invasion
burning sensation blinding explosions tearing
our senses separating families such sudden
atrocities in our ancient cities now crushed
into ash as we ask and plead, why us?

Last Train Out – Forced goodbyes leaving fathers
and husbands behind lost lullabies shrill cries
flooded eyes black skies last kisses uncontrollable
shivers hurried prayers and an infant pining after
her father whilst a grandmother cries out in vain.

Donna Zephrine (USA)
Former combat veteran, Donna works for the New York State Office of Mental Health at Pilgrim Psychiatric Center Outpatient Intensve Case Management. She has had a number of poems published.
E: kauldonna@yahoo.com

UKRAINE POEM

Reading the news
The war in the Ukraine has been going on for twenty days
The newscaster says there may be a possibility of World War III
I think about Iraq and Afghanistan and how for twenty years the US has been at war
I think of Vietnam, Korea, and all conflicts and wars, beforehand,
From being a combat veteran in a hostile environment in Iraq this Ukraine war is giving me flashbacks in combat
The Klitschko Brothers, are Ukrainian former professional boxers one of the brothers being the mayor of Kyiv. They both are not leaving their country as they are proud to fight against the Russians
the people of Ukraine are suffering at the hands of Putin
Ukraine is asking for more aid in supplies and food is scarce
USA is taking in up to 100,000 Ukraine refugees
The devastation of the war is horrific
God Please help this World and the people of Ukraine

Ewith Bahar (INDONESIA)
Ewith is a published author, poet, novelist, translator and essayist. She has published eleven books - in all genres - and her work can be found in more than 80 poetry anthologies worldwide.
E: ewith2408@yahoo.com

THEIR TEARS

My pen quivers
When describing tears
Flows from the river in children eyes
The fast-flowing water
brings the hopes and dreams
to the ocean of nowhere

my pen couldn't stop writing
verse by verse
about their tears and desperation
which intertwine tightly, scream vehemently.

George O. Ndukwu (NIGERIA)
George is a writer and Development Communication specialist from Abuja. His quest in life is to continue doing social good.
E: georgendukwu@gmail.com
Twitter: @george_ndukwu
LinkedIn:@georgw-o-ndukwu-5191795b

'SPECIAL MILITARY OPERATION'

'Special military operation' was his televised address
Launched by him was an 'unprovoked and unjustifiable' war
Across a sovereign and independent country
Vlad the impaler's tanks and troops roared and roamed the streets
A despicable reality across the straits

Ukraine's cities push back in the same vein
Kremlin's attempt to starve them off in the 1930s in vain
Resisting Russian aggression, ashes everywhere
A war eats people, washes them down with blood
I wish I can do more for Ukraine
Now there's a weight on our shoulders
End this war, ultimately for peace to prevail again

Hema Savithri (INDIA)
Hema is a PhD research scholar, novelist and poet. Her works speak aloud for the displaced, marginalized, and the voiceless. She has had a few of her poems published.
E: hemaarikkan@gmail.com
FB: Hema Savithri
Instagram: wordmuse_h

HOPE

March falls like a burst of sunlight
and stands rooted in a corner of our backyard
like a former slave, lonely, beaten on the knees.
My eyes trail the contours of its silence.
We meet. You stare at me.
I at your mournful shadow
that glisten like pure beaded drops
streaming down the cheeks of that little kid
I watched in the television yesterday.
Homeless. Bleeding. Brutally broken.
"Is this what you call war? Nasty!" I hear my son say
as he tosses a ball high up in the air
tearing the borders between unseen worlds.
This is how they kill seasons in mid-air,
kill breath taken from breath shared with love,
kill past, kill hope that winds down
long, dusty roads of history through time,
I hold on to my son's hand.
He raises his head and smiles
at the crazy laughter of the birds
flying above, in the clear blue skies.
I hang prayers on my heart's walls
and pray you've a clear sky overhead.

Jeffrey Marshall (USA)
Jeffrey is a writer, novelist and poet from Arizona. He worked as a journalist and national magazine editor for 35 years. He is the author of four books and a collection of poems.
E: marshwj17@gmail.com
Amazon: @Jeffrey-Marshall/e/B001K8TCC8

ILL WIND FROM THE EAST

A rocket screeches across the night sky
Turns an apartment into rubble, trouble
Is everywhere, hearts trip-hammer in terror
Where is it coming from, and where will it land?
Sirens wail and lights flash red, who will be dead
And who simply maimed? Tank turrets aimed
At Kharkiv and Mariupol, large swaths in ruin
From incessant pounding, the hounding
Of the innocents, those who can only flee.

The line of exiles stretches long, and strong
Uneven as a line etched in the sand by a branch
Dragged by a child. Suitcases and strollers litter the queue
Who will bring safety to the border, create order
From this lumpen mass of human despair? Where
And when will the hot-teared agony end, send
Warm meals and smiles to the bereft?
Relief! Hearts have opened in Poland, planned
Refuge for the sad souls of a shattered land.

Kakoli Ghosh (INDIA)
Kakoli (a.k.a Moon Drops) is based in West Bengal. A post-graduate student in English literature, she has published two poetry books, and her work can be seen in a number of international anthologies.
E: kakolimajumdarghosh@gmail.com
FB: @moon.drops.773
Instagram: @moondrops_2020

DIAMONDS ARE RARE

Out of the snow covered peace
scream my scattered skeleton pieces
yearning through the wuthering winds
to merge into a whole emptiness;
dreamy as truth, proving a real lie.

The flakes of my unconquerable soul
cry as silently as the crucified Love
in the snow sleets of the bleeding sky,
the bat evening hangs upside down
from a parapet of a blasted hospital.

Leaving behind the menaced lanes,
the ruined square that leads nowhere,
I rise out of Love's aborted embryo,
unbowed and imperishable as soul.
I liberate my fate from pit of destiny.

The shards of a broken mirror
never forget to reflect, whatever,
but lies as dangerous as a knife
resting in a crafted scabbard of ages;
as hatred silenced into frozen peace.

Pain, that have not cried aloud,
a flame blown off when still in flicker,
dying, standing in a queue of life
for bread, or melting snow for water,
such stunned deaths deny all horror.

Charged with unwept tear of anguish,
staring eyes of bewildered corpses
turn into diamond in the mass graves;
unearthed coal masters the power,
diamond shapes the ultimate crown.

Karyn J. Powers (USA)
Karyn is based in Wisconsin. She is a published author and poet, and has had work published worldwide. In 1998, she hosted members of a Ukraine government delegations in her home.
E: kjlpowers@aol.com

OLD GLORY

old glory in the colours of a tattered flag
old glory in the choices that the leaders made
old stories spun from envy of what others had
old warriors weaving memories from the long past dead

why does glory always have to come bathed in red
where's the honour in the horror of an ego fed
who's the winner or the loser in what's done and said
what's the difference to those living when we're long past dead

history's written by the winners it is often told
truth is tattered and unravelled in the books we hold
swallowed voraciously or with indifference like a meal gone cold
then fermented in the minds by souls long sold

old glory renders memories of what might have been
old memories warped by warriors block the sins of men
old warriors seeking battles rattle sabres in the wind
old battles yielding bloodshed come alive again

Kathy Sherban (CANADA)
As a recent retiree, Kathy resides in Ontario. She is a poet and author, and her work has been published in several global anthologies and international literary magazines.
E: kmsherban@gmail.com
W: www.kathysherban.ca
FB: @kats_kradle
Instagram: @kat_s_kradle
Twitter: @kathysherban

DAVID VS. GOLIATH

With sirens wailing
bullets rain fear
democracy kneels
freedom disappears
From a sovereign existence
to the battle for Kyiv
a full-scale assault
generations grieve
With innocence lost
they sound the alarm
while the world rallies
a nation's call to arms
Battered by missiles
chins to the floor
broken hearts bleed
from children of war
Human atrocities
a vicious campaign
David vs Goliath
the death of Ukraine

Lauren Mosher (USA)
Lauren resides Virginia and has a career in mortgage. She fulfils her passion of serving others through her volunteer work at the local animal shelter.
E: mosher.laurenmosher@gmail.com
FB: @lauren.brown142892
Instagram: @ilaurenmosher

A MOTHER'S IMPASSE

I rocked my little girl today
And brushed her hair back from her face.
I kissed her nose and smelled her skin;
A moment I won't waste.

I felt the baby in my belly
Move and dance and play,
And whispered to both belly and child:
I'll move mountains to keep you safe.

I think about what it'd be like
If I didn't have a chance
To be present for my babies;
If I had to have a plan.

A strategy of exit
With no notice told at all:
Upon which our lives depend,
No time to think or stall.

What fear I'd feel to leave
The only life I'd ever known,
To trade sweet moments with my children
For armed men threatening my home.

Why are those mothers robbed
Of beholding joy in their child's eye?
For the life of me I cannot figure:
Why be them and why not I?

Keith Burton (USA)
Keith lives in California. As a musician, he has performed throughout the US, and his poems have appeared worldwide. He was honoured to have met Mother Theresa, and the Dalai Lama.
E: keith1080@gmail.com

SAINT JAVELIN OF UKRAINE

I am the saint at the end of the world,
Inviting sinners to darkness.

Trucks scaring our land
Are serpents in Eden.
I shall remove them from Paradise!

My anger is swift:
A jolt of light,
A sudden departure,
Then, the Endless Dark.

Sons and daughters of Ukraine,
Protect our ground and sacred skies.
Shoulder my weight,
Load my arrows,
And give them the gift of light!

Lynette G. Esposito (USA)
Lynette lives in New Jersey. Her poetry has been published in a number of magazines, journals and anthologies.
E: nichecom1@aol.com

MELODY OF THE UKRAINE

I am carrying my cat carrier.
It is heavy and I am tired …
in the Ukraine … running for our life …
the heavy feline is getting heavier.

Air goes in and out of me
like light itself.
I should leave my Melody and go.

She is crying.

I rise, step away from her,
look through the dark
around us.

The earth beneath me struggles to breathe.
Brushing the dirt from my knees,
I open a can of cat food
from my pocket and lick the top
to ease my hunger.
I give the rest to her.
We are on our way again.
Freedom is just a few steps forward.
We will go together.

Ma Jolie Fille (SINGAPORE / INDONESIA)
Ma Jolie Fille - a pseudonym - says that writing helps to release emotions and manage feelings in difficult times, and she believes that with words, all writers have a unique way to express themselves.
E: indahyosevina_mjf@yahoo.com
FB: @ma.b.fille

I STAND AND HUG YOU WITH MY PRAYERS

Blood is no longer red where it should flow freely rather than gasping in cramped veins which need clear oxygen to seduce the lungs.

Tears are no longer seen where they should be as clear as crystallising water rather than mixed with the dust from the flying shell that ravaged our existence.

Isn't it blinding you when the fading blood with the dusty tears mix in the air?
Isn't it dumbed you where the scream of women and children whirl in your very ears?

War, is the arrogance of the leader that should protect and procure peace not change the crystal clear tears into a bloody river.

War, mercilessly destroyed our freedom like flying vultures, they hunger for the flesh, eating you alive!!

War, their hunger is not enough, still not enough to satisfy their thirst until it's broken you into pieces, but I choose to stand by you.

I feel you like I feel my blood boiling under the frozen temperature, I cry for you in unseen tears like a slashing blade touching my skin.

I keep you like every word inked by my old precious pen, I walk with you like a traveller hiking under palpable circumstances.

If my hands are too weary to reach your destination, scattered by the time imprisoned in my spirit, my words are too meaningless for this complicated world, I still choose to stand by you.

Even my body cheated my soul and my heart contending with my head, I will always find a way to stand by you.

In a third of the night, when my energy is consumed by the trials, slowly I am falling into eternity and I am too weak to hold you with my mortality.

How much energy is left?
It's not enough to crawl the arrogant wall, it's not enough to scream the unspoken words and weep the unseen tears.

With all the energy left and all your broken pieces stab to my soul
allow me, unseen but feel,
stand and hug you with my prayers, Ukraine.

Mary Keating (USA)

Mary is a disabled writer and lawyer practising in Connecticut. Her poetry has been published in magazines, journals and anthologies worldwide.
E: mmaryword@yahoo.com
W: www.MKeatinglaw.com
Twitter @MaryKeatingpoet

SOLDIER OFF

A tyrant's power rises from below.
Imagine when he wages war
if every soldier just said, *No!*

Instant peace, even though
not grasped before:
a tyrant's power rises from below.

Imagine hate fallow,
impossible to flourish more
if every soldier just said, *No!*

To follow Father Moscow
the military must ignore their core.
A tyrant's power rises from below

when brother fires countless rounds of live ammo,
kills comrade, mother, sovereign neighbor.
If every soldier just said, *No!*

the world would quash this crazed ego;
and peace might reign forevermore.
A tyrant's power rises from below.
Imagine—every soldier just said, *No!*

Masudul Hoq (BANGLADESH)

Masudul is an award-winning contemporary Bengali poet, short story writer, translator and researcher, and a Professor of Philosophy at a government college. His work has been published around the world.
E: masudul.hoq@gmail.com

INTERVIEW

1.
At one point in the interview
The man remains stable and his cruel eyes!

He said indifferently:
In fact, the flower garden,
There is no difference between the battlefield!

But I was talking about myself
Sitting in the garden, adjacent to his house.

2.
Sitting in the courtyard of the war-torn house
When we are talking
Warplanes are still flying in the sky

A girl brings flowers
The man says in a humble voice:
"She is my daughter;
Her name is Peace".

Matteo Marangoni (ITALY)
Matteo is a tour operator specialising in culture, theatre, music and the arts. He is a writer, author and poet, and has had a number of poems published.
E: matteomarangoni74@gmail.com
FB: @matteo.marangoni.397
FB: @centroletturaarturopiatti
FB: @sudamericanafestival

THE MESHES OF THE EVENING

A guilty idea
is the hypocrisy of current events,
certain words have the same sound
of the steps of the stones.
A child not on time
is not a mild situation
is a calendar where days fall.

Meenakshi Palaniappan (SINGAPORE)
Meenakshi is a literature educator and a quiet observer of the world. She writes to make sense of things. Her poems have been published in magazines, international anthologies and online.
E: meena3.saro@gmail.com
FB: @meenakshi.palaniappan.54

FOR UKRAINE

My heart bleeds for Ukraine,
the refugees created,
the threat of a nuclear war
hanging over our heads.

My heart beats for Zelensky,
the power of his words
to move mountains and
countries to his aid.

My heart yearns for Krishna
to come fight alongside
Ukraine and their leader,
clamp down on this beast that is Putin.

My heart is with all of them –
the lady giving sunflower seeds
to a Russian soldier
so life may bloom where he kills or dies,
the citizens giving captured Russian soldiers
cups of tea, and a phone to call their mothers,
the farmers digging trenches
and patrolling their villages,
the couples who marry and sign up for guns
to defend their country in the same hour,
the soldiers who say
'To hell with you, Russian Warship'
when warned to surrender,
the country that stands now
and hopefully is still standing
tomorrow;

Zelenksy,
who asks Russian mothers
to come claim their sons,
who tells America
he needs ammunition not a ride,

who appeals directly to the Russian people
to speak for him to their president,
who has proclaimed that every square
in Ukraine is Freedom Square,
who has united a divided world
to fight for life to win over death, and
light to win over darkness
the David roaring at Goliath
to learn the word "Reparations,"
the *everyman*
appealing to every man
to see and hear him and his countrymen
fight this war that has landed on his shores ...

Glory be to Ukraine and
Peace onto the world.

Melissa Miles (NEW ZEALAND)
Melissa is an emerging American ex-pat writer living in New Zealand, where she writes in an old cottage overlooking the sea.
E: melissanie59@gmail.com

ESCAPING WAR IN UKRAINE

This weight upon my back
Almost unbearable
But I will endure it
I will carry my friend
My companion
My pet.
You just see a dog
I feel the love roll through my body
From my darling girl
I hold her lovely paws
I stroke them now and then
So she knows I will not desert her.
She is my family and I will not leave her
As so many others did.
Tying their friends to a fence and escaping themselves
Leaving others to pick up the pieces.
Not me.
You have given me so much
I will not leave you in the rubble
Hiding from the bombs and desperate
For food and water
Enduring
This stupid human war
Waged by a dying lunatic
Upon a peaceful nation.
Kind people of the world
Thank you for your help
To hold my head up high
And keep my family with me.

Meri Utkovska (REPUBLIC OF NORTH MACEDONIA)
Meri is a poet, writer and artist. She creates artistic journeys aimed at bringing people closer to their true nature. She has recently published her first book of poetry and photography.
E: m.utkovska@gmail.com
FB: @meriutkovska
Instagram: @marigoldintheether

I STOOD IN SILENCE

I stood in silence
Having failed to contain
Drops and drops of tears to roll away!
So away they rolled,
While silent I stood,
Amidst a handful of mourners -
Amidst a winter-field of graves!
I stood in silence
Having failed to retain
Rivers and rivers of tears to break my soul away,
So away they broke,
While silent I stood
And buried a part of me,
Alongside, with you.

Maria Nemy Lou Rocio (HONG KONG / PHILIPPINES)
Maria started writing poetry when she was in high-school, but only found her way back into writing three years ago as a way of overcoming the trials of being separated from her family.
E: misnemz@gmail.com
FB: @Marias-Corner-My-Poem-My-Story-103973511564918

WE ARE ONE

A minute to pause
To call for peace
Let us be one
No hate, only love

A minute to pause
To call for unity
One world, one voice
Join hands, join hearts

A minute to pause
To break the chain
Of greed, of power
Give end to suffering

A minute to pause
To savour the silence
Let the wounds heal
Breath, forgive, hope, rise

A minute to pause
To reflect and change
Because we are one
We'll remain as one

Peter David Goodwin (USA)
Peter lives in New York, and has worked as a cook, historian, furniture-mover, Bible-salesman and playwright. He spent a year living in Moscow and took several trips to Ukraine.
E: peterdgoodwin@me.com
W: www.peterdgoodwin.net

ONCE, SHE HAD AMBITIONS

She had moved to Moscow
this child of Soviet Society
looking towards the future
this child from a Ukrainian village
who had already lived a lot
whose first husband had her locked
up when she asked for a divorce
who had worked in isolating Siberia—
I am almost thirty, an old woman already
now studying the science of marketing
who had ambitions, many ambitions
but the most visceral was to recover
the two acres and one cow,
stolen from her grandmother
by the Communists.

Where is she now?
Who has survived so many
upheavals—
where is she now?
when Russia tries to steal
her country.

Trish Saunders (USA)
Trish writes poems and short fiction from Seattle, Washington and Honolulu, Hawaii. She has had poems published in a number of journals and publications.
E: plsaunders2@gmail.com

THE YEAR OF THE TYRANT'S FINAL SPRING

I'm standing in a barren garden with Tolstoy, with Chekhov,
and they are frozen in place, like stricken roses of January,
like whipped horses, scarred into silence,
as songbirds with smothered throats.

Until at some signal, a ruckus begins.

Exhausted people walk out of the shadows,
trampling shards of glass,
holding grenades tenderly
as candles.

The poets look at each other, "Do you hear that?"
"Yes," their hands reach for each other.
"It's a chorus of bells."

"And why do they celebrate? Asphalt still smoulders."

"Yes, but a 40-mile convoy through Ukraine
has halted, broken apart like ships,
an army of soldiers is walking home,
accepting flowers from crowds in Kyiv,
courteously ignoring the barbed-wire stems."

The war will go on,
Chekhov and Tolstoy nod to each other.
But this will be the tyrant's final spring.

The words rush away from them into the garden,
I too walk away, wash my hands, read another poem,
concentrate on an enormous sun rising through clouds.

First published in *Open Arts Forum*.

Akua Lezli Hope (USA)
A third-generation New Yorker, with over 400 poems published, Akua uses sound, words, fibre, glass, metal, and wire to create poems, patterns, stories, music, sculpture, adornments, and peace.
E: akualezli@gmail.com
W: www.akualezlihope.com

PRAYER FOR UKRAINE

Because the Cucuteni Trypillia speak
to me across the eons
hips like mine
saying I'm not anomalous
my shape encoded
and arms raised as mine are in celebration
in praise or propitiation
as I both raise and fold them in prayer
now saying, save these people
whose genius I've studied and admire

These people who taught me
in my crippled isolation
who gave me insight
into ways to make my crochet hook dance
and shape bare lines of fibre
into dazzling adornments
new, modern, yet pulling
from the Gaelic past united
with native tradition
that they could reach there
and there and there and there
into fabulous futures
and her and her and me around the world
and free us with their prolific Genius
their energetic creativity
and make community

Weep that those who give so much
are attacked, invaded
the peace and joy of their bursting
growth plucked by covetous minds

I hold you in my heart Ukraine
your city, sister to mine
your bright sovereignty, a beacon
your resolve to remain

must be maintained

Let these words be a prayer
for your protection
a shield against the grasping
jealous reach of foreign tyranny

Let all peace prevail
may every good magic manifest
and embrace you

Let these words be a prayer
may the forcefield of liberty
defend your right to be
deter the destroyers
dismantle the perfidy
deconstruct the undoers

Let these words be a prayer
for your safety and survival

Let these words be a prayer
for restoration and peace.

Michelle Morris (ENGLAND)
Michelle is a South African writer based Devon. She has been writing uplifting, inspiring and thought-provoking poetry all her life, and has been published in a number of poetry anthologies.
E: morrismichelle4@gmail.com
Twitter: @MichellePoet
Instagram: @michellemorrispoet

STAND UP FOR THE GOOD

Mother Russia is crying
Her sons bleed into the earth
Mother Ukraine's sons bleed also
Trying to defend their turf

War is an evil path
Destruction like a hurricane
There are no true winners
Everyone loses in this game

But life and death is not a game
You don't get another life
Putin brings Russia shame
By causing needless fighting

When does it end?
When do we learn from the wars in the past?
What will it take for good men to stand tall
And support what is honourable and just?

History will judge us all
By the decisions that we make
And good men who stand by and do nothing
Are equal in the responsibility stakes

We all want peace and hope
We all want love and freedom
We are more the same than different
We share so much in our faith and meaning

It's time to stand up for the good
It's time to stand up for the right
It's time to be better humans
It's time to support a better life

Mother Ukraine wants to feel safe again

Mother Russia wants to know peace too
All mothers want a future for their children
And all fathers want to realise dreams of truth

Michael H. Brownstein (USA)
Michael lives in Missouri. His latest two volumes of poetry have just been released.
E: mhbrownstein@ymail.com

JUST BECAUSE A LEADER IS MAD DOES NOT MEAN YOU MUST FOLLOW HIM

Putin tries to poke holes into the body's work of a nation
but the body's work of the nation cannot be poked through—

gut-shot punctuation, terrorist renderings, vocabulary of madness
and Russia bleeds fire, cruelty, vocabulary of an insane man's mind.

He walks into the noise more than once,
and now he must exit from the room:

You do not have to follow a leadership lodged in evil.
Following orders is not a defence.

How do you fight a courageous people, Putin?
You do not. Genocide is murder. Murder is murder.

Get out of Ukraine now!

Moinak Dutta (INDIA)
A teacher by profession, Moinak lives at Kolkata. He is the author of two books of fiction and several of his short stories, poems and essays have been published in magazines and journals worldwide.
E: moinakdutta@yahoo.co.in

VIGNETTES OF A WAR

It seemed the whole city had decided to go out
for a tour;
trolleys tugged, children walking holding hands
of parents who looked clueless and tensed,
two blocks away, the same city looked surreal with
not a single soul on the street,
Three yards from the square, scenes got changed
from the surreal to utter desolation,
buildings having big holes, streets having big craters,
black smoke smouldering out of ruins,
a half burnt perambulator, a broken chair,
mangled shape of concrete slabs with iron rods jutting out,

Some thousand miles away from the city
Sitting on his favourite yacht
Someone checked the share prices of certain companies
which specialised in weapon tech,
how green they looked!

Cathy Hailey (USA)
Cathy lives in Virginia. She taught English and Creative Writing at high-school for forty years, and is Northern Region VP of The Poetry Society of Virginia. Her work has been published worldwide.
E: haileycp@gmail.com
FB: @ Cathy Hailey
Instagram:@haileycp
Twitter: @haileycp

Haiku

Border crossing
young boy, two suitcases
push and pull.

PUSHING AND PULLING

The red suitcase he pushes,
nearly as tall as he is,
twice his girth,
holds the weight
of family, country, heritage.

He pulls a second suitcase
behind him, likely his own,
a size appropriate for a young
child, small enough to hold
his clothing, treasures,
memories of home.

Bundled in beanie and coat,
protections from winter freeze,
a hug against inhumanity, he
balances these nimbly as he
crosses the border, emotions
pushing and pulling toward hope
in one direction or another.

Manju Kanchuli Tiwari (NEPAL)
Manju is a clinical psychologist and an eminent writer of poetry, fiction, plays and essays. She has published 18 books, and has delivered poetry presentations worldwide.
E: manjukanchuli@yahoo.com

IN UKRAINE

In a dark day
Black hail showers gun-shells
Angry/defeated acts for victory
Of anarchy and acrimony
O Lord Buddha (god of peace)
Extinguish this devastating fire
Diminish the discriminating borders of hate
Disseminate on earth: Love and order
With your omnipresent blooming light!

How the trust of humanity is crashed
With catastrophe
With missiles and machine guns!
And plane-terror everywhere
In every civilian hearts
Humanity is terrorized
And clogged between the triggers
A line of ants is cynical towards you
"Polluted emotions to kill one another!?
or civilized steps to live together!!??

O liberation!
O self -determination!
O right to survival!
How can people run away from their motherhood
With steps of tears; with heart beats of fear
How can they say 'Bye'?!
Blood - scars over the land
Their unwilling heart steps to move
Wait and see

For a serene: A cool wind blowing sky
A flock of birds: a symbol of peace
We love to see you so much
Flying with full freedom
In Ukraine's beautiful blue sky!

Debi Schmitz Noriega (USA)
Primarily of German and English decent, Debi lives in Iowa. She loves to read, write, collect stamps, design craft books and go to drag racing events.
E: debi_schmitz@yahoo.com

UNTITLED
Her sallow face, frightened eyes,
mussed hair; a slave to terror.
Tiny fingers cling to her slip, under her skirt hem-
For comfort, a silky piece of home.

A broken husband waves goodbye
through his tears and a dust veiled window.
The children, held tightly by mother,
embrace bravery as they stoically wave back.

His family will escape the nightmare
that engulfs the only home they have ever known.
A premonition jolts her as his likeness fads--,
He will die on the streets by our home, alone.

Upheaval of a family by a tyrant with no cause.
One suitcase and stuffed toys clenched in their hands,
she escorts the children to an unknown existence
while wet pearls of grief streak her cheeks.

Julia Paulette Hollenbery (ENGLAND)
Julia lives in London. She is a bodyworker, therapist, mystic, healer, author, teacher and poet, and for over 25 years she's guided clients into deep confidence, intuition and self-authority.
E: julia@universeofdeliciousness.com
W: www.universeofdeliciousness.com
Instagram: @julia.paulette.hollenbery
Twitter: @juliahollenbery

RESILIENCE, WAR & PEACE

Unbelievable!
It doesn't make sense
Cruel
Unfair
Unprovoked
Hurtful

I can not imagine
Your shock, fear and terror
Loss and grief
Jumping out of normal bodily calm
As attacking tanks advance
And bombs loudly explode
Turning home into dusty rocks.

We watch from afar,
Our ordinary lives full of petty details,
Washing-up, squabbles with neighbours and bills to pay,
Saluting your awesome collective courage -
Proportion delivered now here
And how can we possibly help you?

We none of us know how we might respond
Under such intense provocation.

May you be reunited,
Women and children with your men.
Families, communities, neighbourhoods again.
May the children know, it's not their fault.
May your architecture and civilization be rebuilt.

Cry, shake, shout and stamp,
And sleep to deeply rest.
Let the trauma, frustration and anger move through
Cushioned by love from a stunned world

Be soothed, you are seen, your story is known.

My heartfelt wish is that your crisis,
This danger is also an opportunity
A wake-up call for the world
To realize peace is essential inside and out.
Your losses not chaos but sacrificed
Ultimately for a global greater good.

May your pain be healed
Rubble rebuilt into new beauty
Tragedy turned into transformation
Cruelty stopped.

Putin, traumatized child of post-war tragedy
Revisiting traumatic war
And so it unconsciously goes on...

Ukraine
May you find the ways to heal
To stop the transference
Of pain
Generation to generation.

Bowing
To your courage. You roar!
May you find safety and recovery.

Phoenix from the flames
Regeneration
And resource
Transmuting pain to gold.
You will thrive with dignity and humanity
Finding peace in your hearts
And pleasure in your bones.

Elizabeth Harmatys Park (USA)

Elizabeth lives in Wisconsin, and is a sociologist, teacher, prison volunteer, and poet. She has published three chapbooks, and her poetry has been published in numerous journals and anthologies.
E: parkeliz@yahoo.com

HELPLESS

What about the children?
Who will keep them safe?
How can they get home?
I lost them in the crowd
They were swept away
while I am pushed along
streets full of strangers,
up stairs, through buildings
I don't know where I am

or where I am going
I don't know this city
Maybe I could find a car or
someone to drive me home
but I have nothing, no money
I want to ask someone for help
but no one understands me
no one pauses no one stops
Everyone keeps moving fast

No one knows me
No one cares

Michael Rollins (ENGLAND)
Michael teaches at the Furness Academy in Barrow in Furness, Cumbria, and has lived for a short while in Kyiv. He cannot think of a better reason or cause for writing poetry than to support Ukraine.
E: mikeyrollins@yahoo.com
FB: michael.rollins.90857

SCREAM

Scream on your birthday
Scream all your life
Scream if you're a husband
Scream if you're a wife

Screams for the defenceless
Screams for the poor
Screams from a tower
Screams from a sewer

What I was promised
Was more than I hold
The future was mine
I was young, I was bold

Now I scream at the walls
At the bullet and gun
I scream at tomorrow
And every day to come

I scream at injustice
I scream for the dead
I scream at the leaders
And where I was led

And all I was promised
Was more than I hold
The future was mine
I was young, I was bold

Scream with me now
While protest is allowed
Screaming isn't screaming
If your head is bowed

Church bells are ringing
Out in the square

No one is listening
No one is there

And all I was promised
Was more than I hold
The future was mine
I was young, I was bold

So scream with me
A Banshee roar
Like you have never
Screamed before

Your screams reach the sun
They fill the sky too
Scream for the yellow
Scream for the blue

And all I was promised
Was more than I hold
The future was mine
I was young, I was bold

Marilyn Peretti (USA)
Marilyn lives in Illinois. She is active in several poetry writing groups and regularly attends reading sessions. workshops and festivals around the world. Her work can be seen in a number of journals.
E: marilynperetti@yahoo.com
W: www.perettipoems.wordpress.com

VERONIKA

Sweet baby girl
is born amongst shelling
and destruction of
the city of Mariupol,
her mother barely escaping
the maternity hospital,

rushing down broken
stairs, her belly bulging
with this bursting infant.

One more strike
by the twisted Russian
President, trying to
recreate the old
Soviet Empire,
painfully bringing
back ancient history,

and they name her
Veronika,
"bringer of victory."

Moushumi Bhattacharjee (INDIA)
Moushumi lives in the eastern part of India, and is a published writer and author, and regularly contributes to various national and international newspapers, magazines, e-zines and anthologies.
E: moushumi54321@gmail.com
FB: @Moushumi's Sphere
Instagram: @Moushumi146

BATTLE OF EGOS

Kings are in rage
A war deadly staged
Bombs and artillery
Raining in fury
Like a house of cards
Towns and cities falling apart
Peace talks are gathering moss
Gulping savagely breeds and barns
Reverberating around yells and cries
Terror-stricken are innocent lives
Sickening stench of charred flesh
Throws civilized society in a trash
Bewildered commoner's pale gaze
Demands an end of the bloody rampage
Peace talks are gathering moss
Kin of dead incurs the loss.

Monsif Beroual (MOROCCO)

Monsif is a multi-awarded and internationally renowned poet. His poems have been translated into 11 languages and published in more than 300 international anthologies and magazines.
E: monsifberoual@yahoo.com
FB: @Monsif Beroual

HUMANITY PREVAILS, NOT WARS

Military forces around the globe,
Teach me how to be
A soldier ready to go
in long nights
in cold days
A machine, waiting for an enemy
For unknown battle
A fight shall come one day
A loss of war waiting for both sides,
On my shoulder holding a rifle gun
A bullet ready to pull out
The First bullet, killed my humanity
The Second one killed my root as a human being,
Around me there are no enemies
Just poisoned words control me
Sorry sir, my gun not ready
Because on this globe, there are no enemies
There is only one family
Shaped into different colours
With different beliefs
Separate into different nations
And only love shall prevail
To embrace all one day, not wars.

Naida Mujkić (BOSNIA AND HERZEGOVINA)
Naida received her PhD from the Faculty of Philosophy. She has published seven books of poetry, edited several others, and her work has appeared in literary journals and anthologies around the world.
E: naida.mujkic@yahoo.com
FB: @naidamj

THE DOUBLE

Every time I walk into
My father's room
His face is waiting for me
Like a heavy cloud full of rain

He is sitting in front of the TV
And watches the
Ukrainian channel
Even if he doesn't
understand the language

He waves his hand
Trying to scare the flies away
From the coffee table

They say every man in the world has
seven doubles
But my father has only one

An ex-soldier
sitting in front of the TV
until he sees
A face more horrified than his own

Nandita De (INDIA)
Based in Kolkata, Nandita is a writer, senior editor, freelance journalist and poet. She has co-authored 42 anthologies, and has had work published in a large number of magazines and journals.
E: nanditade@gmail.com
FB: @Nandita De
Instagram: @Nandita.De
Twitter: @NanditaDe1

YESTERDAY ONCE AGAIN

Millions at peril
Who destined it so?

Greed and avarice
Unsatiated thirst for power

Mankind at its worst
Madness at its peak

Brothers! They called us
And bombed us in sleep

Never were they enemies
Not one a threat to the attacker

A war which can never be justified
A war which can never be forgiven

Far away in Kyiv
In a country locked between two foes

Lived a happy lot
Without ill will to the world

Now millions fleeing in the night
Forced refugees in the mindless fight

Civilians forced to take up arms
Young medicos taking flight

Students cloistered in bomb shelters
In the aftermath of a pandemic and the approaching platoons

Will they reach the borders?
Will man, woman and child survive?

Will the neighbouring nations shelter
Give them new lives?

What will tomorrow bring?
For citizens who've suddenly lost their sleep?

What new horrors will unfold
As bloodthirsty troops run amok?

Tanks rumble in
Crushing cars and a country's hopes

Horrified, the world just bystanders
Watching the show

Common men, respectable citizens
Brought to the crossroads

It's 2022, but terror still reigns
Man killing man without an end

Naseha Sameen (INDIA)
Naseha lives in Hyderabad, and is a Data Scientist by profession. She has been published in over 20 anthologies, and has won a number of awards for her work.
E: naseha.s@gmail.com
W: www.naseha.world
FB: @StoriesbyNaseha
Twitter: @nasehasameen

HEROES OF THE WAR

Heroes of the war will be rejoiced later when the war is done.
Millions homeless, thousands of dead; countless broken homes.

Songs will be sung again of valour, of heroism, of courage
Amidst invisible broken lives, a villain and a hero will emerge.

History pens down the victor as the hero;
Atrocities, as necessary controls for greater good.

Truth lies injured, fatally in the blood wrenched soil,
Slowly fading from lives and memories forever, lost.

Nattie O'Sheggzy (NIGERIA)

Nattie has been writing poetry and short stories for more than two decades. He has published two poetry books, and his works have appeared online and in anthologies worldwide.
E: nattie4all@yahoo.com

YELLOW & BLUE

Yellow and blue
        two lively hues
                twilight and sky
rain soaked but why

Winter of love
        to pull or shove
                the ticking clock
with painless pocks

Yellow or blue
        the wintery hues
                reflect the sky
don't ask me why.

Email intrusion
        tells emotions
                hidden in the dark
crevices arc

Yellow and blue
        bomb may be cool
                with your arm strong
Dying flame is long

Steps on the ice
        feeble feet thrice
                search for lost arms
there comes the harm

Yellow and blue
        colours askew
                harvest of tears
basket of flares.

Neal Whitman (USA)
Neal lives in California and supports UNICEF. Neal's grandfather was one of the Ukrainian Whitmans who escaped the Czarist draft in 1905. Neal's school-yard nickname was Walt.
E: neal.pgpoet@gmail.com

VICE VERSA
☐
displacement of hostility
well-known psychological term
for redirecting aggression
from original source to
a less threatening recipient —
for example, kicking the dog,
rather than your over-bearing boss

hostility of displacement
resentment expressed when,
pushed into express train,
you exit, no longer pursued
by a bear, and you bid farewell
to what was your Jerusalem —
prognosis is weeping by the river

Neha Bhandarkar (INDIA)
Neha is an author and translator, and a columnist for a Marathi newspaper. She has published 13 books in Marathi, Hindi and English, and has received a number of awards for her work.
E: nehabhandarkar65@gmail.com

A HOME IN UKRAINE

I had built a house ...
A house by bricks
A house by hands
A house by hearts
Our house was a perfect home

There were open windows
Doors, trees and
Fragrance of flowers
Fresh air used to touch
my heart
We were happy in our home
We were living in the era of
'Revolution Of Dignity'

Chirping of birds
The melody of rivers
The symphony of sea waves
The beauty of nature
Everything has lost
In the war

24th February was the day
Russia started Special Operation
Now not only the homes but
Green corridors are not safe for us
Ukrainian have faced
Terrifying situation after
The attack on Zaporizhazhia
Nuclear Power plant
The Earth even trembled
By this act

Now we are living but not alive
We are not dead but deprived of life
We are inhabitants of Ukraine
But homeless now

I don't know
When I can build a home again now

Nivedita Karthik (INDIA)
Nivedita is a graduate in Immunology from the University of Oxford. She is also an accomplished Bharatanatyam dancer and published poet. She resides in Gurgaon.
E: nivedita5.karthik@gmail.com

RISING TALL

A dusky pink blanket with a large hole
    dusky from the grey clouds of ash and smoke
drapes the arm of a couch
in what was once a home but is now an empty shell
with dolls and cutlery strewn about.

A new father, holding his daughter,
    his daughter born of war and fire
weeps for this new being
who is born into a world without love
yet looks so much like the love he just lost.

A child on the run turns around one last time
    one split second
to look at his beloved school.
One second too long
for ashes now cover the ground
the ground that is shrouded by a swirling grey blanket.

And yet

A metro station is now a home
a home to countless thousands
a home where each word is interspersed by a blast
a home where every second counts as a miracle of life
a home where, in the corner, by what were once glass windows,
one Sunflower grows proud and tall.

Nolo Segundo (USA)
Nolo lives in New Jersey and taught in the war zone of Cambodia. He only became a published poet as he neared his 8th decade, but has since had poems in published 35 literary magazines worldwide.
E: nolosegundo70@gmail.com

WHEN EVIL BREATHES ...

When evil breathes,
it breathes out the air of death,
killing children's innocence,
pulling apart lovers and
sinking the old into despair.

When evil invades a nation, it
destroys cities house by house,
laying waste to museums and
schools and hospitals and all
the places where the people
go to worship God... but-
evil is stupid, evil is foolish,
thinking it can escape itself,
until discovering that all
it has done has delivered it
to hell.

Onoruoiza Mark Onuchi (NIGERIA)
Onoruoiza is a Corporate Communications Consultant based in Lagos. His poetry can be seen across a wide range of global platforms and anthologies.
E: markonuchi@gmail.com
Instagram: @markpoet
Twitter: @markpoet

THE PAIN OF MOURNING

Grief is grey
hounding lobes -
you lyre
to the Stygian mix:
a verse you etch
on the edge
of bursting gloom
to torrid clouds
of endless waterworks!
The clammy sun
mortifies your gait
with grails of gloom
the void is cold
clumping loud
to your vinyl!
The unbundling rhythm
pales the Muse
on niggling storm.
The screen unveils
the trail of wails
bullets, bombs, and bile
smoulder the scenes
Ukraine in flames
PEACE-
Unfold thyself!

Pamela Brothers Denyes (USA)
Recently retired, Pamela based in Virginia Beach. Her first two collections,were published in 2022, and her award-winning poems appear in multiple journals and international anthologies.
E: pamelabrothersdenyes@gmail.com

A BLUE AND YELLOW FLAG

Exodus shifts a nation's people westward.
    With no peril involved, I drive westward from my home.
Afraid to run, a mother cannot find food for the children.
    In Virginia, a pair of finches pulls fluff for a spring nest.
Bodies queue up on the square, still in acrid smoky air.
    Here, a fly walks safely toward my coffee cup.
He's a famous American who had to walk to get out of Ukraine.
    Beyond my window, a deer walks, safely grazing.
Their president vows to stand and fight with his people.
    Today I will stand on a mountain's ledge praying for him.
Thirteen children killed by aggression, so far–war crimes!
    Fly lands on the glass door; I have no taste for killing today.
Russian troops hover like flies on a still-warm carcass.
    Raise the fly-swatter, Europe, and clear the air!
Everybody has a reason not to challenge a dictator.
    A hunting hawk circles above the mountain's tree line.
Democracy careens downward, nothing to stop it, save the bottom.
    Supportive sunflowers swarm social media.
Apartment buildings burn and crumble to the square.
    I will do more than fly a blue and yellow flag.

Pankhuri Sinha (INDIA)
Residing between New Delhi and Muzaffarpu, Bihar has had two poetry collections published in English, and five poetry collections published in Hindi, and many more lined up in both languages.
E: nilirag18@gmail.com

WHERE IS THE CEASEFIRE?

Where is the ceasefire?
The one so loudly announced
By the aggressor
With the claim of being human
To the whole world
Aghast, enraged
Focused on containing the war
Before ending it
Waiting, eagerly waiting for the ceasefire
Agreed upon mutually
Amidst repeated calls for diplomacy
Yes, that ceasefire
Where is it?

That ceasefire, which would stop
The raining artillery
The constant shelling
The unending fire in the sky
Falling on the ground
Exploding in orange burning flames
Destroying the beautiful skyline of
That loveliest of nations
Ukraine! Liberal and mannered
Rich and cultured
Famed and pretty
With the sea green minarets
Golden domes of Kyiv
An era, generations really
Lives being reduced to rubble
Being hastily buried in mass graves
Open air a suspected place
As hospitals and schools
Theatres and bunkers
All are bombed
With new weapons each day
Where is that ceasefire?

Patrick O'Shea (NETHERLANDS)
Patrick is both British and Dutch and lives in Rijswijk. Recently retired, he finds writing to be a most satisfying part of his life, and has had a number of pieces published.
E: patrick@copas.demon.nl

THE HORROR GOES ON

The horror goes on, and I feel ashamed as I watch this perverted destruction of life,
A university burns In Kharkiv after a missile strike, a small hospital also damaged,
In Zhytomyr buildings burn after another attack and more civilians are seen to be dead,
And the impotency I feel grows as the horror and the unjustified killing goes on and on.

What is now happening is so very reminiscent of old footage I have seen of cities in WW2,
Yet here we are in 2022, and an ongoing systematic attempt to extinguish freedom continues,
I fail to understand how any Russian troops can participate in the unprovoked slaughter,
Have they lost any sense of humanity as a tank turns and deliberately fires into an apartment?

Does it really matter if the sense of humanity seems to have been removed from the invaders?
I am left feeling sick at what I am seeing, but cannot ignore it, know I must remember this,
Remember the horror, and remember the Ukrainian courage, and the faces of the refugees,
But also remember those in so many bordering countries who offer aid and some peace.

The horror goes on, bodies shown on Russian tv lie in a wood people may have enjoyed last week,
Tanks roll through so many cities, can they really believe they liberate anything in shelling,
Can they really liberate people who stay to fight for their country, no liberation ever needed,
The horror goes on, and I am so ashamed of this lack of humanity, the deaths, and the losses.

Patty Walnick (USA)
Patty lives in Dallas and sees writing as both an outlet and potential avenue towards touching others in an effort to simultaneously validate emotions and spread healing light.

NATASHA NATASHA

Natasha, Natasha
Your light grows dim
The shine in your eyes is shadowed and still
I see the tear you're desperately holding back on the brim

Sadness hides behind a stoic gaze
Worry lingers like a smoky haze
Fear churns deep inside

Mother oh Mother, what is to become of you?
Father's head hangs low
Crying, as he well knows, he cannot protect his brood
What will become of us all?

Natasha, Natasha, you are the emblem of Ukraine
Beautiful, strong, drowning in love, drowning in pain

The World empathizes
The World Understands
Reaching to help with shackles on their hands

Like a paralysed body unable to move
The spirit works to find a way
Embraced by strangers
Encouraged by nations
Lifted and loved in the midst of the fray

Let us help you rise
As you stand tall and full with fight
Accept our encouragement, dance in our light
Together in oneness we can escape the night

Paul Parker (ENGLAND)
Paul is a retired war Veteran and lives in Shropshire in England. War has long inspired his poetry.
E: flakjacket80@yahoo.co.uk

ANGEL

The Angel of Death glides down to rest upon the cusp
Of the Earth.
Her face, a study in bone and flesh, taut as steel.

Wings of black, framed like a giant bat, leathery with strength.
Sinewy, massive in aspect.
Talons gleam in razored reflection.

She looks down upon the Earth, seeking out souls expectant.
War and Famine, Cruelty and Hate.
A smile upon a face beautiful evil.
"Come children come. Death becomes you all".

The Angel of Death, a mother that awaits a dying breath.
With a whisper jubilant, she crooks her Song of Death.

Peter W. Morris (USA)
Peter is an International Photojournalist, and has worked in 75 countries on six continents, many having been visited repeatedly.
E: pbjmissions@gmail.com

MY WORDS, MY WEAPONS

I am a soldier, therefore I kill
Sometimes in anger at life's injustices
But never in hatred
I am a man under orders
Yet my words are my weapons
Not a flicking of the forefinger
Sending projectiles unto death
Brothers, sisters, children…victims
Family, global relatives, Russians
Late at night, under cover of canvas
A sky colourfully streaked with death
Evidence of bombs, bullets, battalions
My mind wanders to distant times
People and places I have known
Happiness and sadness, joy and pain
I prop up on my cot, pen in hand, paper close
A poem is composed in flickering shadows
"So long I've waited, to touch your face
Breathe deeply of your scent alone
Taste the salt upon your cheeks"
Out of my sleepless conscious, letters
"Dear One, as the sounds of conflict envelops
My world, I recall our last goodbye
At the train station, as you and the children
Escaped to Poland, to safety
Our words come to me in this dreadful place
Where friends die, yet I survive
Loneliness is my constant companion
I seek God's solace
"All things work together for good …"
Understanding is difficult
I will sleep, fitfully, my words my consultation
I write, therefore I am

Rebecca K. Leet (USA)
Rebecca lives in Virginia. She was a journalist and writer throughout her career, but not a poet until retirement. She has been published in various journals and anthologies, and her first book was recently published.
E: rebeccaleet@gmail.com

NO TIME TO CHANGE SHOES

All I could see was the shoe
on her left foot, a high heel –

spiked but not stiletto –
dark colour, appropriate for office wear.

Had she had time, no doubt,
she would have gone home and changed to sneakers –

more appropriate for broken field running
away from the Russian Army.

But she didn't have time
which is why I saw the classic pump

jutting out of a tarp neighbours used
to carry her and lay her gently

in a trench
with others who hadn't had time.

Rebecca Sutton (NEW ZEALAND)
Rebecca is a part-time writer from Auckland. Currently studying English after studying for her bachelor's in Fine Arts, Rebecca's aim is to tell a story with her poetry.
E: rsut80@yahoo.co.nz

UNTITLED – A RESPONSE ABOUT UKRAINE

Never, never thought I
review so long as without end.
People bustling and bringing around
running, running, into what?

The trees don't seem to matter
when conflict takes over.
Two days, the hours merge into one
as the dogs wander by alone.

Salutations are never as easy
seeing rabble and red is never pleasing
A flag changes and changes back again
All I really want is water and grain.

It's a shame, it really is
it could be all wonder and bliss.
Sun shining from a canopy sky
teeth widening and it doesn't even try.
Will this end, will it ever?
Hard to say, blackness can be forever.

Sobhna Poona (SOUTH AFRICA)
Sobhna is a writer and poet living in the Eastern Cape.
E: sobhna.poona@gmail.com

RISE

surreal dawn
jolts
from restless dreams
snow falls on
blackened boughs
and vacant playgrounds
where hopes burgeoned before
we fell asleep to
exploding lies from
invading bombs
memories splinter
day - night #- candlelight
we brace for the menace
of mad men and missiles
when daylight comes
we will collect flowers
walk with our dogs
and hug strangers
on the tendrils of spring
where hope flows
in swathes of yellow and blue

Ranjit Sahu (USA)
Ranjit resides in Virginia. He is a poet, author, and columnist, and writes semi-technical articles for various magazines. He has published three books of poetry.
E: sahurkcutm@gmail.com

UKRAINE BURNING

Undeterred by the torrents of gun fires,
Kiev puts up a valiant fight, standing tall.
Results of the human fears and desires,
Another war upon mankind befalls.

Inevitable is a war; for peace,
Not easy though to stand tall, not be cowed.
Each moment is a fight till the guns cease
Bombs boom and missiles target aloud,

Ukraine burns as cities get scorched and scarred-
Rubbled into graves and mixing with sand.
None who loves humanity, supports war-
Injustice against free life shall not stand.
Nations rise with new power: post clashes,
Growing like a phoenix from their ashes.

Rubilyn Bollion Cadao (HONG KONG / PHILIPPINES)
Rubilyn is Filipino, and works as a domestic worker in Hong Kong. She started writing poems when she was in high-school; writing about love, nature and life's struggles.
E: rubilyncadao1@gmail.com
FB: @dux illinois

FOR TOGETHER WE STAND

Walk on with the faith in your heart
Though your dreams are shattered apart.
Hold your head up high with your hope.
Together we stand on the slope.

Never lose hope and keep going.
Hold onto your faith; keep praying.
Don't be afraid, you're not alone.
Together we stand, we belong.

At the end of the storm appears
A rainbow in the sky declares,
A new and peaceful beginning,
Unity and peace unending.

For together we stand along
With hope and faith we all belong.
For together we wish and pray,
For a better place we could stay.

END

ALSO FROM THE POET

We produce some of the largest international anthologies on particular themes and topics ever published.

CULTURE & IDENTITY: Volumes 1 & 2
ADVERSITY: Volumes 1 & 2
FRIENDS & FRIENDSHIP: Volumes 1 & 2
FAITH: Volumes 1 & 2
CHILDHOOD: Volumes 1 & 2
CHRISTMAS – SPECIAL EDITION
A NEW WORLD - Rethinking our lives post-pandemic.
ON THE ROAD: Volumes 1 & 2
WAR & BATTLE
THE SEASONS
LOVE

www.ThePoetMagazine.org

Printed in Great Britain
by Amazon